WEALTH REIMAGINED

Transforming Your Finance with Generative AI

DR. OLADIPUPO JUDE MESOLE

TABLE OF **CONTENTS**

INTRODUCTION

THE IMPORTANCE OF FINANCIAL MANAGEMENT IN A DIGITAL ERA

Managing money has always been a vital part of life, but in today's fast-changing world, financial management is more critical than ever. With technology advancing at lightning speed, our financial decisions have become more complex, and the stakes are higher. People no longer rely solely on cash and ledgers; we now live in an era of online transactions, credit cards, digital wallets, and even cryptocurrencies. This shift has made managing finances a skill that everyone must master to avoid falling behind.

Historically, financial management was relatively straightforward. Most people balanced their checkbooks, saved a portion of their income, and planned for significant expenses, such as buying a house or retiring. Today, the story is very different. We have an abundance of financial tools and opportunities at our fingertips, but with them come new challenges. For example, markets now move faster, expenses are harder to predict, and debt can pile up quickly if not managed properly. As the financial world becomes increasingly digitized, the need for clear and intelligent decision-making has grown exponentially.

The digital era has also introduced a flood of data into our lives. Every purchase we make, every subscription we sign up for, and every investment we consider generates data. While this data holds the potential to help us better understand our financial habits, it can also feel overwhelming. Without the right tools, many people struggle to make sense of it all, which often leads to poor financial choices or missed opportunities.

This is where technology plays a pivotal role. Tools like mobile banking apps, budgeting software, and even basic artificial intelligence have already started transforming how we handle our finances. These tools help simplify tasks like tracking expenses, setting savings goals, or paying off debts. Yet, even with these advancements, gaps remain. These traditional tools often focus on analyzing the past—what you've spent, how much you've saved, and where you went over budget. But what about looking forward? What about helping you predict challenges or identify opportunities before they happen?

This is the critical moment when Generative AI steps into the spotlight. Unlike traditional financial tools, which focus on reviewing what's already occurred, Generative AI is about creating possibilities for the future. It analyzes patterns in your financial behavior, considers the broader economic environment, and generates strategies tailored to your specific goals. Whether it's identifying areas where you can cut back on spending or suggesting investments that align with your values, Generative AI offers solutions that traditional tools simply can't match.

The importance of financial management in the digital era extends beyond simply balancing a budget or accumulating wealth. It's about gaining control in a world where economic uncertainty is more prevalent than ever. With economies shifting rapidly and job markets becoming more unpredictable, being proactive in managing your finances can make the difference between stability and struggle. This era has redefined financial success—not just as the ability to earn money but as the ability to manage it wisely, grow it responsibly, and secure it against risks.

The rise of online marketplaces, freelance work, and side hustles has also added new dimensions to financial management. For example, more people are earning income from multiple sources, which creates opportunities but also complicates tax planning and long-term savings. Without a clear plan, managing such diverse income streams can quickly become a source of confusion. At the same time, businesses are facing mounting challenges, from global competition to fluctuating markets. Entrepreneurs and corporate leaders must now manage their finances with greater precision, ensuring that every dollar spent contributes to their goals.

Generative AI not only simplifies these complexities but also enhances your ability to plan for the future. Imagine having a financial advisor available 24/7, one who doesn't just review spreadsheets but generates real-time insights tailored to your unique situation. For instance, if your expenses unexpectedly increase one month, the AI could suggest adjustments to your budget or recommend areas where you could save. If you're looking to grow your investments, you might analyze market trends and simulate potential outcomes to guide your decisions. These aren't distant possibilities—they're already happening.

In this digital era, time is one of our most valuable resources, and effective financial management enables us to conserve it. Instead of spending hours manually tracking expenses or trying to understand tax laws, you can rely on tools that do the heavy lifting for you. This efficiency gives you the freedom to focus on other essential aspects of your life, like spending time with family, advancing your career, or pursuing your passions.

As we navigate this new era, the importance of financial management cannot be overstated. It's not just about numbers; it's about building a life of security and opportunity. When managed well, finances can become a source of empowerment rather than stress, a tool to achieve your dreams rather than a limitation holding you back. Generative AI, as we'll explore in this book, is the key to unlocking this potential.

The digital era has redefined what's possible in personal and business finance. Whether you're an individual trying to save for a down payment on a house, a freelancer juggling multiple income streams, or a business owner aiming to optimize operations, the stakes are high. But with Generative AI on your side, the challenges of financial management in a digital world can transform into opportunities for growth, efficiency, and long-term success.

THE ROLE OF GENERATIVE AI IN TRANSFORMING FINANCIAL STRATEGIES

Generative AI represents a revolutionary advancement in the realm of technology, particularly in its ability to redefine financial strategies for individuals, small businesses, and global enterprises. Traditional financial management often relies on reactive decision-making, where analysis occurs only after data have been collected and events have unfolded. Generative AI, however, brings a proactive dimension to the table, generating insights, forecasts, and actionable strategies that empower decision-makers to anticipate and adapt to financial challenges before they arise.

At its core, Generative AI operates through advanced models such as Generative Adversarial Networks (GANs) and Transformer architectures, which can process and synthesize vast amounts of data. These models not only analyze historical patterns but also create new pathways for financial growth and resilience by simulating possible outcomes and identifying previously untapped opportunities. For instance, in stock market investments, Generative AI can simulate thousands of market scenarios, enabling investors to understand potential risks and rewards across various strategies.

One of the most transformative aspects of Generative AI lies in its ability to democratize access to high-level financial intelligence. Historically, access to sophisticated financial advice and tools was limited to wealthy individuals or large corporations that could afford professional consultants and advanced software.

Generative AI changes this dynamic by offering affordable, scalable solutions that cater to a broad audience. From personalized financial planning to risk assessment, these AI-driven tools are now accessible to anyone with an internet connection, leveling the playing field for individuals and small businesses.

Personalized Financial Strategies

Generative AI excels at creating tailored financial strategies, taking into account a user's unique goals, spending habits, income streams, and market conditions. Unlike generic financial tools that rely on static templates, Generative AI continually learns from a user's financial behavior, updating strategies in real time. For example, a freelancer with irregular income can benefit from a dynamic budget generated by AI, which adapts to fluctuating earnings and expenditures. Similarly, long-term investors can rely on AI-generated portfolios aligned with their ethical values, risk tolerance, and financial milestones.

Moreover, Generative AI offers an unparalleled level of precision in financial forecasting. By analyzing a combination of historical data, economic indicators, and market trends, it is possible to predict changes in interest rates, stock prices, or consumer spending patterns. These predictions allow users to make informed decisions, whether it's timing an investment, adjusting savings plans, or preparing for economic downturns.

Streamlining Financial Operations

In the corporate world, Generative AI is revolutionizing how businesses manage their financial operations. It automates routine tasks such as expense tracking, invoice processing, and payroll management, freeing up valuable time and resources. Additionally, it provides businesses with advanced tools for financial modeling, enabling them to explore various scenarios and make data-driven decisions. For instance, a startup seeking funding can utilize AI to simulate the financial impact of various business models, enabling them to present stronger cases to investors.

Risk management is another area where Generative AI demonstrates its transformative power. Financial risks often arise from market volatility, unforeseen expenses, or inefficiencies within an organization. Generative AI identifies these risks by analyzing patterns and anomalies in real time, suggesting actionable solutions to mitigate potential losses. For example, it might flag an impending cash flow issue for a business and recommend cost-cutting measures or alternative revenue streams before the problem escalates.

Revolutionizing Investment Strategies

Generative AI's impact on investment strategies is profound. Unlike traditional investment tools that analyze past data to predict trends, Generative AI models can simulate future market conditions, allowing investors to test the viability of their strategies under various scenarios. For example, an AI tool might simulate the effects of geopolitical events, regulatory changes, or emerging technologies on a portfolio, providing investors with a clearer understanding of potential outcomes.

Furthermore, Generative AI enhances the capabilities of robo-advisors—automated platforms that manage investment portfolios. While conventional robo-advisors focus on diversification and risk management, those powered by Generative AI offer more sophisticated insights, such as identifying undervalued stocks or predicting optimal entry and exit points for trades. This level of granularity enables both novice and experienced investors to optimize their portfolios with confidence.

Enhancing Savings and Wealth Accumulation

Generative AI has also transformed savings strategies. Traditional savings plans often follow rigid structures, which can fail to adapt to changing financial circumstances. Generative AI introduces a dynamic element to savings, creating plans that adjust to variations in income, expenses, and financial goals. For instance, it might allocate more funds to savings during periods of high income and reduce contributions during leaner months, ensuring that financial goals remain attainable without unnecessary strain.

Generative AI also aids in wealth accumulation by identifying hidden opportunities for financial growth. It might recommend investment options tailored to an individual's risk profile or suggest tax-efficient strategies to maximize returns. These personalized recommendations enable users to build wealth sustainably while minimizing unnecessary risks.

Fraud Detection and Security

Security is a critical component of financial management, and Generative AI plays a pivotal role in safeguarding assets. By constantly monitoring transactions and account activities, AI models can detect irregular patterns that may indicate fraud or unauthorized access. For instance, an AI system might flag a transaction that deviates significantly from a user's usual spending behavior, prompting immediate action to prevent potential losses. As cyber threats become increasingly sophisticated, Generative AI continues to evolve, offering robust defenses against fraud and enhancing the overall security of financial systems.

Empowering Financial Independence

Ultimately, the transformative power of Generative AI lies in its ability to empower individuals and businesses to achieve financial independence. By automating complex processes, generating innovative solutions, and providing real-time insights, Generative AI removes barriers to effective financial management. It encourages proactive decision-making, enabling users to take control of their finances with confidence and clarity.

Whether it's creating a retirement plan, navigating volatile markets, or optimizing tax strategies, Generative AI provides the tools needed to succeed in an increasingly complex financial landscape. By embracing this technology, users can not only achieve their financial goals but also redefine what is possible in the world of finance. This transformation is not just about efficiency; it's about empowerment, allowing everyone to thrive in the digital era.

OBJECTIVES AND AUDIENCE

The financial world is evolving rapidly, and staying ahead requires not just awareness but action. This book, "Transforming Your Finances with Generative AI," is more than a guide—it's a bridge connecting traditional financial methods to the innovative possibilities offered by cutting-edge technology. The aim is to simplify complex concepts and demonstrate how Generative AI can be a powerful ally in achieving financial success, whether on a personal or business level.

The primary objective of this book is to demystify Generative AI and show how it can directly impact financial strategies. Many people hear about AI and think of futuristic robots or highly technical algorithms, but this book takes a practical approach to the subject. Generative AI isn't just for tech experts; it's a tool anyone can use. From creating flexible budgets to crafting detailed investment strategies, Generative AI empowers users to take control of their finances with clarity and precision.

WHAT THIS BOOK AIMS TO ACHIEVE

Educate

At its core, this book aims to educate readers about Generative AI. Many people are familiar with AI in general—tools like voice assistants or automated chatbots—but Generative AI is a unique subset. It can generate entirely new solutions based on learned patterns, making it incredibly useful for solving complex financial challenges. This book breaks down these advanced concepts into understandable terms, ensuring every reader, regardless of their technical background, can grasp the potential of this technology.

Provide Practical Applications

Theory alone isn't enough. This book bridges the gap between knowledge and action by offering step-by-step guidance on how to use Generative AI tools effectively. Each chapter is packed with real-life examples and actionable tips to help readers integrate AI into their financial practices. Whether it's automating savings, forecasting investment outcomes, or managing risks, the focus remains on practical value.

Empower Decision-Making

One of the most significant challenges in financial management is making informed decisions. People often struggle to choose the right investment, balance their budgets, or plan for unexpected expenses. Generative AI changes the game by offering insights and recommendations tailored to individual needs. This book equips readers with the tools to confidently take charge of their finances, ensuring they are prepared for both opportunities and challenges.

Encourage Ethical Use of AI

While the potential of Generative AI is immense, it's essential to approach it responsibly. This book addresses critical ethical considerations, such as data privacy, bias in AI systems, and compliance with regulations. By understanding these aspects, readers can utilize AI in a manner that is both effective and respectful of broader societal implications.

WHO THIS BOOK IS FOR

This book is designed for a broad audience, reflecting the universal need for better financial management. It doesn't matter if you're an individual trying to manage your budget, a small business owner aiming to cut costs and increase profitability, or a seasoned professional looking to explore the newest financial technologies—this book has something valuable to offer.

Individuals Seeking Financial Independence

For those who feel overwhelmed by their financial responsibilities, this book provides practical tools to regain control. It demonstrates how Generative AI can simplify everyday tasks, such as tracking expenses or planning for the future, making financial management less intimidating and more achievable.

Entrepreneurs and Business Owners

Business owners face constant pressure to make the right decisions, whether it's about managing cash flow, investing in growth opportunities, or mitigating risks. Generative AI can act as a virtual financial advisor, offering insights that would typically require an entire team of experts. This book offers guidance on leveraging AI to remain competitive in a rapidly evolving market.

Financial Professionals

Even experienced professionals can benefit from the advanced capabilities of Generative AI. This book introduces tools and techniques that enhance analysis, improve forecasting accuracy, and streamline financial operations. It's a valuable resource for staying ahead in a field that's becoming increasingly technology-driven.

Anyone Curious About Technology and Finance

Lastly, this book is for anyone with an interest in the intersection of technology and finance. Whether you're curious about how AI works or want to understand its implications for the future, this book provides insights that are both informative and engaging.

WHY THIS BOOK MATTERS

Financial decisions profoundly shape our lives, influencing everything from the quality of our daily experiences to the legacy we leave for future generations. In an era where technology touches every aspect of our lives, understanding and leveraging Generative AI isn't just beneficial—it's essential. This book is your roadmap to navigating this new frontier, combining timeless financial principles with the latest technological advancements.

The goal is simple yet ambitious: to equip you with the knowledge and tools needed to thrive in an increasingly digital financial landscape. By the end of this book, you will not only understand Generative AI but also feel confident in applying it to your financial goals, unlocking opportunities that were once out of reach.

This isn't a book filled with abstract ideas—it's a practical, hands-on guide designed to inspire action. Whether you're planning for the future, seeking to optimize your current finances, or exploring innovative business strategies, this book will show you how Generative AI can make a meaningful difference in your financial journey.

CHAPTER 1

UNDERSTANDING GENERATIVE AI

DEFINITION AND CORE CONCEPTS

Generative Artificial Intelligence (Generative AI) is a cutting-edge subset of artificial intelligence designed to create new data, content, or solutions by learning from patterns in existing datasets. It differs significantly from traditional AI, which primarily focuses on analyzing data to make decisions, predict outcomes, or perform classifications. Instead, Generative AI takes a creative leap by producing original outputs that are indistinguishable from those created by humans.

For example, while traditional AI might analyze your expenses and categorize them into fixed and variable costs, Generative AI could go further by generating a dynamic budget that adjusts to your real-time financial behavior. Similarly, in market analysis, traditional AI identifies trends, whereas Generative AI simulates potential scenarios, helping stakeholders visualize the impact of their decisions in diverse conditions.

The concept of Generative AI stems from the fundamental idea of mimicry—learning how to emulate the complexities of human thought, decision-making, and creativity. By training on vast datasets, these AI systems can synthesize unique solutions to complex problems, whether it's composing an email, creating artwork, or developing financial strategies tailored to specific needs.

HOW GENERATIVE AI DIFFERS FROM TRADITIONAL AI

To appreciate the uniqueness of Generative AI, it's essential to compare it with traditional AI. While both are subsets of machine learning, their purposes and methodologies diverge:

Traditional AI:

Analyzes and interprets existing data to make predictions or decisions.

Typical applications: fraud detection, data classification, and process automation.

Example: An AI system might analyze historical stock prices to predict future trends.

Generative AI:

Creates new data based on learned patterns, enabling innovation and driving further advancements.

Typical applications: creating financial models, simulating market scenarios, and crafting personalized financial plans.

Example: A Generative AI system doesn't just analyze stock trends but generates potential scenarios, helping investors test strategies under hypothetical conditions.

Generative AI's ability to produce new outputs unlocks possibilities in areas where creativity, adaptability, and foresight are critical.

The Philosophy Behind Generative AI

Generative AI embodies a revolutionary principle: using data not just as a resource but as a foundation for creation. Its operation reflects a three-step process:

- Learning: Absorbing large datasets to understand underlying patterns and relationships.
- Synthesizing: Using these patterns to create something new, such as a predictive model or a personalized strategy.
- Refining: Continuously improving outputs through feedback and iteration.

In finance, this philosophy enables Generative AI to:

- Understand Complex Dynamics: It learns intricate relationships within markets, customer behaviors, and financial ecosystems.
- Create Adaptive Solutions: Whether it's a retirement plan or a tax-saving strategy, the outputs evolve with changing data.
- Iterate and Optimize: AI systems adapt over time, ensuring their recommendations remain relevant and actionable.

KEY CHARACTERISTICS OF GENERATIVE AI

Generative AI systems share several defining characteristics:

1. Versatility: Capable of generating diverse outputs such as text, images, financial models, and market predictions.
2. Adaptability: Continuously learns from new data, ensuring outputs remain relevant.

3. Efficiency: Automates complex, time-consuming tasks, enabling rapid decision-making.
4. Creativity: Produces solutions and insights that may not be intuitive to humans.

For example, a Generative AI-driven financial assistant could predict optimal investment opportunities by synthesizing data from historical trends, current market conditions, and user preferences. This type of creative insight gives users a competitive edge in managing their finances.

GENERATIVE AI AND HUMAN-LIKE CREATIVITY

One of Generative AI's most compelling features is its ability to mimic human creativity. This is made possible by its foundational models, which include Generative Adversarial Networks (GANs), Variational Autoencoders (VAEs), and Transformer-based architectures. These technologies, discussed in detail later in this chapter, enable AI to move beyond data processing to data creation.

For instance:

In text generation, Generative AI can draft personalized financial reports with language and tone indistinguishable from that of a human.

In image generation, it can visualize data trends as infographics tailored to user preferences, enhancing accessibility and comprehension.

Real-World Example: Generative AI in Financial Planning

Consider Sarah, a young professional seeking financial stability. Traditional AI might categorize her expenses and recommend saving 20% of her income monthly. Generative AI, however, goes further:

- Dynamic Budgeting: It tracks her real-time spending and adjusts her budget based on changes in income or unexpected expenses.
- Scenario Simulation: It generates multiple savings plans, simulating outcomes like an economic downturn or a salary increase.
- Personalized Insights: By analyzing Sarah's goals—buying a house, paying off student loans—it crafts strategies tailored to her unique needs.

Such capabilities showcase the potential of Generative AI to revolutionize personal finance.

EXPANDING FINANCIAL OPPORTUNITIES

Generative AI's transformative nature lies in its ability to uncover opportunities and optimize strategies that were previously inaccessible. For businesses, this means identifying untapped markets or refining operational efficiencies. For individuals, it means gaining insights into managing their finances with precision and foresight.

For example:

- Investment Strategies: Generative AI can create hypothetical market scenarios, enabling investors to prepare for various potential outcomes.
- Risk Assessment: It identifies subtle risks that traditional systems might overlook, enabling preemptive action.
- Goal Alignment: AI dynamically adjusts financial plans to keep users on track, even amid changing circumstances.

As technology advances, these capabilities will only grow more sophisticated, empowering users to achieve unprecedented levels of financial efficiency.

KEY TECHNOLOGIES: GANS, VAES, AND TRANSFORMERS

Generative AI derives its strength from cutting-edge technologies like Generative Adversarial Networks (GANs), Variational Autoencoders (VAEs), and Transformer-based architectures. These systems work together or independently to provide the creative, analytical, and adaptive power that defines Generative AI. In this section, we will explore the mechanics, applications, and transformative impact of these technologies, particularly in the financial sector.

Generative Adversarial Networks (GANs)

Introduced by Ian Goodfellow and his team in 2014, GANs

represent one of the most influential developments in artificial intelligence. GANs consist of two competing neural networks—the generator and the discriminator—that engage in a zero-sum game, refining their outputs over time.

Mechanics of GANs

The Generator: This network creates synthetic data samples by learning patterns from the input data. For instance, in finance, it might generate synthetic stock market data or simulate economic conditions.

The Discriminator: Acting as a quality control mechanism, the discriminator evaluates the generator's output against real-world data and provides feedback. The generator uses this feedback to improve its outputs iteratively.

This adversarial relationship ensures that the generator produces increasingly realistic data over time. Imagine a GAN creating synthetic trading scenarios based on historical market fluctuations. The discriminator evaluates these scenarios, enabling the generator to refine its ability to accurately mimic market conditions.

Applications of GANs in Finance

GANs hold transformative potential in the financial sector. Some notable applications include:

- **Market Simulation:** By generating realistic market scenarios, GANs allow investors and institutions to test various strategies in a risk-free environment.

- **Fraud Detection:** GANs generate potential fraud patterns, enabling systems to identify and combat fraudulent activities preemptively.
- **Portfolio Stress Testing:** GANs simulate worst-case economic conditions, helping portfolio managers assess and mitigate risk effectively.

Example

A hedge fund might use GANs to simulate a stock market crash. By exposing their portfolios to these simulated conditions, fund managers can prepare strategies to minimize losses in real-world crises.

Variational Autoencoders (VAEs)

Variational Autoencoders are powerful tools for data compression and representation learning. They excel at encoding complex datasets into a compressed format and reconstructing them, making them invaluable for uncovering hidden patterns and generating new data.

Mechanics of VAEs

Encoding Phase: The input data is transformed into a latent space representation—a compact, abstract version of the original data.

Decoding Phase: The latent representation is reconstructed into the original or a modified form, enabling the generation of new data samples.

The key feature of VAEs lies in their ability to learn probabilistic representations, ensuring that outputs are not only accurate but also varied. This variability is beneficial in financial forecasting and personalized planning.

Applications of VAEs in Finance

- **Anomaly Detection:** By learning the typical patterns of financial transactions, VAEs can detect deviations that may indicate errors or fraud.
- **Customer Segmentation:** VAEs analyze customer behavior to identify distinct financial profiles, enabling the provision of tailored service offerings.
- **Risk Assessment:** By modeling the distribution of financial data, VAEs provide insights into potential risks and opportunities.

Example

A financial institution could use VAEs to analyze customer spending habits. By detecting anomalies, such as sudden spikes in credit card activity, the system can flag potential fraud.

Transformer-Based Architectures

Transformers are the backbone of modern Generative AI systems, particularly in tasks requiring sequence processing, such as natural language generation and analysis. Their innovative self-attention mechanism has revolutionized how machines process data.

Mechanics of Transformers

Transformers work by processing input data as sequences and understanding the relationships between elements within those sequences. Their self-attention mechanism allows them to focus on the most relevant parts of the data.

- Self-Attention: This enables the model to weigh the importance of each data point about others. For example, in a financial report, the transformer might emphasize revenue trends over ancillary details.
- Multi-Head Attention: Transformers split the attention mechanism across multiple dimensions, allowing the system to analyze data from various perspectives simultaneously.

Applications of Transformers in Finance

Financial Document Analysis: Transformers extract insights from complex reports, such as earnings statements or market analyses, providing actionable recommendations.

Market Trend Prediction: By analyzing sequences of historical data, transformers can forecast market movements and identify emerging trends.

Automated Customer Support: Transformers power AI chatbots that interact with customers, providing real-time financial advice and support.

Example

A bank might use transformers to automate the generation of personalized financial plans. By analyzing a customer's transaction history, the system could recommend investment opportunities or savings strategies tailored to their goals.

Integrating These Technologies

While each of these technologies offers unique strengths, their true power lies in integration. A financial AI system might use transformers for analyzing textual data, VAEs for segmenting customer profiles, and GANs for simulating market conditions. Together, they create a comprehensive framework for tackling complex financial challenges.

The capabilities of GANs, VAEs, and transformers are constantly evolving. Researchers are exploring hybrid models that combine the strengths of different approaches, such as GAN-transformer hybrids, for enhanced content generation. In finance, these advancements could lead to even more sophisticated applications, such as real-time financial forecasting and fully autonomous portfolio management.

APPLICATIONS IN FINANCE

Generative AI is not merely a tool for efficiency—it is a groundbreaking technology reshaping the financial landscape. Its ability to analyze vast amounts of data, identify patterns, and generate novel solutions provides unparalleled opportunities for predictive analytics, personalized financial planning, and fraud detection. These applications transform the way individuals and businesses make decisions, mitigate risks, and achieve financial goals.

Predictive Analytics

One of the most potent applications of Generative AI in finance is its ability to forecast trends with a degree of accuracy and insight that surpasses traditional methods. Predictive analytics, powered by Generative AI, enables financial institutions, investors, and businesses to anticipate market movements, assess risks, and make data-driven decisions with confidence.

Generative AI models, such as those based on Transformer architectures, excel at identifying subtle patterns within vast amounts of historical financial data. Unlike conventional models, which rely on predefined assumptions, Generative AI learns dynamically, adapting to the complexities of real-world markets. This adaptability allows it to uncover insights that might otherwise remain hidden.

For example, in stock market analysis, Generative AI can process years of historical trading data, market news, and even geopolitical events to identify correlations and predict how specific stocks or sectors might perform under certain conditions. An investor leveraging this capability can act on trends early, gaining a competitive edge.

Beyond the stock market, Generative AI has been instrumental in economic forecasting. Governments and multinational corporations utilize predictive analytics to forecast macroeconomic shifts, including inflation rates, unemployment trends, and global supply chain disruptions. These forecasts enable proactive measures, from policy adjustments to resource allocation, ensuring better preparation for potential economic turbulence.

Generative AI also plays a crucial role in portfolio management by simulating various market scenarios and stress-testing investment strategies. By evaluating potential risks and rewards under different conditions, financial planners can provide clients with recommendations that are not only robust but also adaptable to unforeseen market changes.

In 2022, a leading asset management firm adopted Generative AI to enhance its forecasting capabilities. By integrating GANs (Generative Adversarial Networks) into its models, the firm could predict the effects of interest rate hikes on bond markets with 20% greater accuracy than traditional methods. This enabled the firm to adjust its portfolio in advance, achieving higher returns for its clients.

Personalized Financial Planning: Crafting Strategies Unique to You

Generative AI is redefining personalized financial planning by making it more accessible, accurate, and adaptive. Unlike traditional financial tools that rely on static inputs and rigid structures, AI-driven solutions are dynamic, offering tailored strategies that evolve with an individual's financial journey.

At the heart of this transformation is the ability of Generative AI to analyze vast datasets, including spending habits, income patterns, financial goals, and even external economic factors. This comprehensive analysis allows for the creation of truly individualized financial plans that maximize opportunities while minimizing risks.

For instance, an AI-powered financial advisor can help a young professional create a savings plan by analyzing their monthly expenses, identifying unnecessary expenditures, and suggesting realistic goals. As the individual's financial situation changes, such as receiving a raise or incurring unexpected costs, the AI can adjust the plan in real-time to maintain alignment with long-term objectives.

Generative AI also excels at breaking down complex financial concepts into actionable insights. For example, instead of overwhelming a user with detailed market data, it can provide simple, digestible suggestions, such as "Increase your retirement contributions this month by $100 to stay on track for your long-term goals."

This personalized approach extends beyond individual finances to small businesses. For entrepreneurs, Generative AI can assess cash flow patterns, inventory levels, and market conditions to recommend strategies for optimizing operations and increasing profitability. By tailoring solutions to a business's unique needs, AI ensures that resources are allocated efficiently, enabling sustainable growth.

The adaptability of Generative AI also makes it an invaluable tool for underserved populations. Many people avoid traditional financial advisory services due to high costs or complexity. Generative AI bridges this gap by offering affordable, easy-to-use tools that democratize access to financial planning. For example, mobile apps powered by AI can guide users in creating budgets, setting savings goals, and investing responsibly, empowering them to take control of their financial futures.

A 2023 study highlighted a fintech startup that used Generative AI to offer personalized financial coaching. The AI analyzed users' historical financial data, providing daily updates on spending trends, investment opportunities, and savings goals. Over six months, 70% of users reported improved financial health and a 15% increase in their savings rates.

Fraud Detection: Securing Finances in a Digital Age

The rise of digital transactions has made the financial sector more vulnerable to fraud, cyberattacks, and unauthorized activities. Generative AI is at the forefront of combating these threats, offering solutions that are both proactive and adaptive.

Unlike traditional fraud detection systems that rely on predefined rules, Generative AI continuously learns from new data, improving its ability to identify unusual patterns or anomalies. This approach allows financial institutions to detect and mitigate fraudulent activities before they escalate.

For example, consider a scenario where an individual's credit card is used to make a huge purchase in a foreign country. While a rule-based system might flag this as suspicious, Generative AI takes it a step further by analyzing the context, including the individual's travel history, recent transactions, and even the time of day. If the AI determines that the transaction aligns with the user's typical behavior (e.g., they are currently traveling abroad), it might approve the transaction. On the other hand, if inconsistencies are detected, the AI can immediately block the transaction and alert the user.

Beyond detecting fraudulent transactions, Generative AI enhances overall cybersecurity by simulating potential attack scenarios and identifying vulnerabilities. For instance, GANs can be used to create synthetic data that mimics real-world fraud attempts. This data is invaluable for training systems to recognize and respond to emerging threats, ensuring that security measures remain effective even as cybercriminals develop new tactics.

Fraud detection powered by Generative AI also benefits small businesses and startups, which often lack the resources for sophisticated security systems. By integrating AI-driven tools, these organizations can protect themselves from threats without incurring significant costs. For example, an AI-powered payment processing system can monitor transactions in real-time, flagging any suspicious activity and preventing potential losses.

In addition to protecting assets, Generative AI plays a critical role in building trust. Financial institutions that adopt advanced fraud detection systems can offer customers peace of mind, enhancing their reputation and fostering loyalty. This trust is crucial in today's digital-first economy, where concerns about data breaches and identity theft are at an all-time high.

In 2021, a multinational bank implemented Generative AI to enhance its fraud detection systems. The technology identified and prevented over $10 million in fraudulent transactions within the first year, with a 95% reduction in false positives compared to traditional systems.

Ethical Investing and ESG (Environmental, Social, and Governance) Strategies

While not in the original outline, ethical investing is another area where Generative AI shines. By analyzing vast amounts of ESG data, AI can help investors align their portfolios with their values. For instance:

- Data-Driven Decisions: Generative AI generates reports on companies' environmental impact, helping investors avoid businesses with poor sustainability practices.

- Risk Mitigation: AI identifies long-term risks associated with unethical practices, safeguarding investments.

The applications above demonstrate how Generative AI not only enhances decision-making but also transforms financial systems. By offering real-time insights, personalized strategies, and unparalleled security, it empowers both individuals and institutions to navigate complex financial landscapes with confidence.

In subsequent chapters, this book will explore how these applications can be effectively implemented in budgeting, investing, and long-term planning, providing a roadmap for leveraging Generative AI in every aspect of financial management.

CHAPTER 2

BUDGETING WITH GENERATIVE AI

AUTOMATED EXPENSE TRACKING

Managing personal finances often begins with tracking expenses, but for many, this can be a tedious and time-consuming task. Generative AI streamlines this process by automating the tasks of sorting, analyzing, and categorizing expenses. Through advanced algorithms, it not only tracks where your money goes but also provides insights that can help improve spending habits. Let's explore how automated expense tracking powered by Generative AI works and why it's becoming an essential tool for better budgeting.

THE NEED FOR AUTOMATED EXPENSE TRACKING

Keeping track of daily expenses is vital for maintaining financial control, but traditional methods often fail to capture the whole picture. Manual tracking, whether through notebooks, spreadsheets, or basic apps, requires constant attention and effort. It's easy to miss small purchases, overlook patterns in spending, or forget to log transactions altogether. This creates gaps in understanding, making it more difficult to adhere to a budget or identify where adjustments are necessary.

Automated expense tracking eliminates these challenges. By using Generative AI, financial tools can now monitor your spending in real-time, categorize transactions automatically, and even offer suggestions to optimize your budget. This means you no longer have to input data yourself or spend hours analyzing where your money is going. Instead, you receive an accurate and up-to-date financial overview with minimal effort.

(Pouyan Parsafard, Ogerta Elezaj, Damilola Ekundayo, and Edlira Vakaj, 2024) How Generative AI Powers Automated Tracking Generative AI relies on advanced machine learning models trained to recognize patterns in financial data. Here's how the process works:

Transaction Monitoring:

Generative AI connects to your bank accounts and credit cards through secure channels. It monitors all transactions—deposits, withdrawals, purchases, and transfers—and compiles them into a centralized system.

Categorization of Expenses:

The AI identifies the nature of each transaction based on merchant details, amounts, and your previous spending habits. For example:

- A purchase at a supermarket is classified as "Groceries."
- Payments to a gym are listed under "Fitness."
- Subscriptions like Netflix are grouped as "Entertainment."

Real-Time Updates:

The tracking occurs in real-time, ensuring your financial data is always up-to-date. As soon as a transaction is recorded, it's categorized and reflected in your expense tracker. This allows you to make adjustments immediately if needed.

Insights and Alerts:

Over time, Generative AI learns your spending patterns and provides insights. It might alert you if you're exceeding your usual budget in certain categories or if a recurring charge has increased. These alerts help you stay on track without having to sift through data yourself.

Benefits of Automated Expense Tracking

Automated expense tracking offers more than just convenience; it transforms how people manage their money.

1. Time-Saving: Manual logging of expenses can take hours each month. With AI, this process is instant. You simply link your accounts, and the system handles the rest.
2. Accuracy: Human errors, such as forgetting to record a purchase or mislabeling an expense, are common in traditional tracking methods. Generative AI eliminates these mistakes by automating the process.
3. Comprehensive Overview: AI captures every transaction, no matter how small. This ensures you have a complete picture of your finances, helping you identify where most of your money goes.
4. Actionable Insights: Instead of just showing numbers, AI-powered trackers interpret data. For instance, it might suggest reducing

dining out if a significant portion of your income is spent on restaurants.

5. Customizable Categories: Unlike static systems, Generative AI allows you to customize expense categories based on your preferences. For example, if you have a hobby like photography, you can create a category specifically for related expenses.
6. Stress Reduction: Knowing your finances are being tracked accurately and automatically reduces the mental burden of budgeting. You can focus on your goals instead of worrying about missing details.

FEATURES OF AI-DRIVEN EXPENSE TRACKING TOOLS

Several financial tools and apps now use Generative AI to enhance their expense tracking capabilities. These features make them stand out:

1. Integration with Multiple Accounts: Most AI tools support integration with multiple bank accounts, credit cards, and even investment accounts. This consolidates all your financial data in one place.
2. Recurring Payment Detection: Generative AI can identify subscriptions and recurring payments. It helps users manage these better by providing reminders or suggesting cancellations for services no longer in use.
3. Spending Trends Visualization: AI trackers often include

dashboards with graphs and charts that show spending trends over weeks, months, or years. This visual representation makes it easier to spot patterns.

4. Language-Based Queries: Some advanced tools, like those powered by chat-based AI, allow users to ask questions about their spending. For example, you can ask, "How much did I spend on groceries last month?" and get an instant answer.
5. Security Features: Given the sensitivity of financial data, these tools prioritize security and data protection. They utilize encryption and other security measures to ensure that user information remains confidential.

REAL-LIFE EXAMPLES OF AUTOMATED TRACKING IN ACTION

The impact of Generative AI on expense tracking is best understood through real-life applications. Here are some examples of how individuals and businesses have benefited:

Personal Finance Management:

Sarah, a freelance graphic designer, used to struggle with managing her irregular income. After integrating an AI expense tracker into her routine, she could easily categorize her spending, identify periods of higher expenses, and plan accordingly. Over time, the tracker helped her save 20% more by suggesting areas to cut back.

Family Budgeting:

A family of four started using an AI-powered budgeting app to manage household expenses. The app automatically tracked their grocery bills, utility payments, and discretionary spending. By showing the family their highest expense categories, they were able to reduce unnecessary purchases and allocate more funds towards savings.

Small Business Use Case:

A café owner relied on AI for expense tracking to manage operational costs. The tool identified inconsistencies in supply costs, alerting the owner to negotiate better deals with vendors. This not only improved profitability but also streamlined financial reporting.

ADDRESSING CONCERNS ABOUT AUTOMATION

While the benefits of automated expense tracking are undeniable, some users have reservations. Common concerns include:

Data Privacy:

Sharing financial data with an app can feel risky. However, most AI-driven tools use secure encryption to protect sensitive information. It's important to choose platforms with a proven track record of safety.

Over-Reliance on Technology:

Some worry that automating expenses might make them less aware of their spending habits. To counter this, many tools include features that encourage users to review and manually approve categories or adjustments.

Learning Curve:

First-time users may find it challenging to navigate AI-powered apps. Thankfully, most tools offer tutorials and support to ease the transition.

FUTURE OF AUTOMATED EXPENSE TRACKING

As Generative AI evolves, expense tracking tools are expected to become even more innovative and more intuitive. Future developments might include:

- **Predictive Adjustments:** Tools that automatically adjust budgets based on upcoming expenses, like annual insurance premiums.
- **AI-Powered Financial Coaching:** Beyond tracking, AI could offer personalized advice on achieving financial goals.
- **Voice and Gesture Controls:** Hands-free options for managing expenses via smart devices.

These innovations will continue to simplify personal finance management, making financial literacy and stability more accessible to everyone.

CREATING DYNAMIC, ADAPTIVE BUDGETS

A budget is a plan for managing your money effectively. Traditionally, people have used static budgets that are fixed and only change when manually adjusted. However, life is unpredictable—expenses fluctuate, incomes change, and unexpected events arise. Generative AI has introduced a solution to these challenges: dynamic, adaptive budgets. These budgets evolve in real-time, responding to changes in your financial circumstances and goals. This section examines how Generative AI can enhance budgeting by making it more flexible, effective, and personalized.

Dynamic Budgeting

Dynamic budgeting is a process where your budget changes automatically based on real-time data. Unlike static budgets, which remain the same until manually updated, dynamic budgets adjust as your financial situation evolves. For example, if your income increases, your budget might allocate more toward savings or investments. Conversely, if an unexpected expense arises, the budget reallocates funds from less critical areas to cover the cost.

Dynamic budgets are like having a financial advisor available 24/7. They don't just tell you what you spent; they help you adapt and plan proactively.

How Generative AI Creates Adaptive Budgets

Generative AI plays a crucial role in making dynamic budgets possible. Here's how it works:

Analyzing Income and Expenses

Generative AI first analyzes your income sources and spending patterns. It tracks where your money comes from and where it goes. For example:

- Income streams, such as salaries, freelance work, or side hustles.
- Expenses like rent, groceries, subscriptions, and entertainment.

The AI continuously updates this data, ensuring it has a clear and current understanding of your financial situation.

Predicting Future Changes

Using patterns in your financial data, Generative AI predicts future changes. For instance:

- If your utility bills are higher in winter, the AI adjusts your budget to prepare for increased heating costs.
- If your income typically rises during holiday seasons, it anticipates this and reallocates funds to savings or other priorities.

These predictions help you stay prepared, even for seasonal or irregular changes.

Setting Real-Time Priorities

Based on your goals, the AI adjusts your budget in real-time. For example:

- If you want to save for a vacation, the AI identifies areas where you can cut back, such as dining out or entertainment, and redirects those funds to your savings goal.
- If an emergency expense arises, like a medical bill, it reallocates money from non-essential categories, such as clothing or travel, to cover the cost without derailing your financial plan.

Benefits of Dynamic Budgets

Dynamic budgets powered by Generative AI offer numerous advantages:

Flexibility

Life is unpredictable. A static budget might fail when unexpected expenses arise, but a dynamic budget adjusts to keep you on track. For example, if your car breaks down, the AI reallocates money from other categories to cover the repair costs, ensuring you don't fall behind on your goals.

Efficiency

Manual budgeting can be time-consuming and prone to errors. Generative AI handles the heavy lifting, automatically updating your budget to ensure it accurately reflects your current situation. This saves you time and ensures accuracy.

Goal-Oriented Planning

Dynamic budgets are not just about managing day-to-day expenses; they help you achieve long-term goals. Whether it's saving for a down payment on a house, paying off debt, or building an emergency fund, the AI ensures your budget aligns with your objectives.

Stress Reduction

Money management can be stressful, especially when facing unexpected expenses. A dynamic budget reduces this stress by proactively adjusting to changes, ensuring you remain financially stable.

REAL-LIFE EXAMPLES OF DYNAMIC BUDGETING

1. Sarah's Journey to Financial Stability

Sarah, a freelance graphic designer, had an irregular income that made budgeting difficult. She started using a budgeting app powered by Generative AI. The AI:

- Tracked her monthly income variations.
- Adjusted her budget during low-income months, prioritizing essentials like rent and groceries.
- Recommended saving extra during high-income months to build a cushion for leaner times.

After a year, Sarah had saved enough to cover three months of expenses, giving her financial peace of mind.

2. David and Emily's Family Budget

David and Emily, a young couple with two kids, struggled to manage their growing expenses. By integrating Generative AI into their budget:

The AI identified unnecessary subscriptions they had forgotten about, such as an unused gym membership.

It adjusted their grocery budget based on seasonal discounts and family needs.

When their car needed repairs, the AI reallocated funds from their vacation savings temporarily, ensuring they didn't dip into emergency savings.

Their budgeting process became more efficient, and they achieved their financial goals more quickly.

3. Small Business Example: Local Café

A small café used Generative AI to manage its operational budget. The AI:

Predicted seasonal changes in customer demand and adjusted inventory spending.

Recommended reallocating funds to marketing during slow months to attract more customers. Suggested cutting back on non-essential expenses like decorations during high-expense periods.

The café not only stayed afloat but also increased its profitability by 20% within a year.

HOW GENERATIVE AI LEARNS AND ADAPTS

Generative AI doesn't just create budgets; it learns and improves over time. Here's how:

Learning from Your Behavior

The AI observes your spending patterns, learning which categories fluctuate and which remain constant. For example, if your grocery expenses rise during the holidays, the AI anticipates this in future budgets.

Responding to Feedback

Many AI-driven budgeting tools allow users to provide feedback. If you categorize a transaction differently or change a goal, the AI incorporates this information to improve its recommendations.

Integrating External Data

Generative AI also takes into account external factors, including economic trends, inflation rates, and seasonal price fluctuations. For instance, if gas prices rise, the AI adjusts your transportation budget accordingly.

Dynamic Budgeting Tools

Several tools use Generative AI to create adaptive budgets. Here are a few examples:

- **YNAB (You Need a Budget):** Focuses on helping users allocate every dollar to a specific purpose while allowing for adjustments.
- **Mint:** Offers real-time tracking and personalized recommendations based on spending patterns.
- **Pocket Smith:** Uses AI to forecast future cash flow and adjust budgets accordingly.

These tools empower users to take control of their finances without the hassle of manual adjustments.

Challenges and Considerations

While dynamic budgeting with Generative AI offers many benefits, it's essential to be aware of potential challenges:

Data Privacy

Your financial data is sensitive. Ensure that the AI tools you use prioritize encryption and secure storage to protect your information.

Overreliance on AI

While AI is a powerful tool, it's essential to stay engaged with your finances. Regularly review your budget to ensure it aligns with your personal values and goals.

Initial Setup

Setting up an AI-driven budget may require time and effort, particularly for users unfamiliar with the technology. However, this is a one-time investment that pays off in the long run.

The Future of Dynamic Budgeting

As Generative AI continues to evolve, dynamic budgeting will become even more advanced. Future developments may include:

- Voice-Activated Budgeting: Imagine asking your AI assistant, "How much can I spend on dining out this week?" and receiving an instant response.
- Hyper-Personalization: Budgets tailored not just to your finances but also to your lifestyle and preferences.
- Integration with Wearables: Financial updates delivered directly to your smartwatch or fitness tracker, keeping you informed on the go.

The possibilities are endless, making budgeting more accessible and effective for everyone.

CASE STUDIES ON SUCCESSFUL AI-DRIVEN BUDGETING

Generative AI has transformed the way people manage their finances by providing personalized, efficient, and adaptive solutions. While it's easy to talk about the potential of AI in theory, real-world examples truly showcase its value. This section presents detailed case studies, highlighting how individuals and businesses have successfully integrated Generative AI into their budgeting processes. These examples illustrate not only the practical applications of AI but also the tangible benefits it delivers.

Case Study 1: Lisa's Debt-Free Journey

Lisa, a high school teacher in her late 30s, had always struggled with budgeting. Despite her stable income, she found herself drowning in credit card debt due to impulse shopping and poor financial planning. She decided to use a budgeting app powered by Generative AI.

Problem Identification

The AI tool analyzed her spending habits by connecting to her bank accounts. Within minutes, it identified recurring unnecessary expenses:

- Subscriptions she no longer used.
- Excessive spending on online shopping.
- Weekly overspending on dining out.

Personalized Recommendations

Based on this data, the AI tool suggested a step-by-step plan:

- Cancel non-essential subscriptions.
- Set a weekly limit for dining out.
- Redirect saved money toward her credit card payments.

Dynamic Budget Creation

The AI created a budget tailored to her income and goals. It prioritized debt repayment while ensuring she had enough for essentials and occasional treats. Each month, the budget automatically adjusted based on her income fluctuations and spending patterns.

Results

Within two years, Lisa managed to pay off 70% of her debt. She praised the AI-driven tool for its consistent support, saying, "It felt like having a financial coach in my pocket."

Case Study 2: John's Family Vacation

John, a father of two, wanted to save for a family vacation without sacrificing his family's comfort. However, he found it challenging to set aside money consistently. He turned to an AI-powered budgeting app for help.

Tracking Hidden Expenses

The AI reviewed his financial history and identified several hidden costs:

- Overlapping streaming service subscriptions.
- High utility bills could be reduced with better planning.
- Weekly grocery overspending due to unplanned purchases.

Smart Savings Plan

The AI proposed a savings strategy:

- Automatically transfer a fixed amount to a dedicated vacation fund every payday.

- Suggest cheaper alternatives for groceries without compromising quality.
- Monitor and alert John if his spending exceeds the set limit for any category.

Encouragement and Updates

The app sent encouraging updates about his progress, such as "You're 50% closer to your goal!" This kept John motivated to stick to the plan.

Outcome

By following the AI's advice, John saved enough money in just 11 months for a memorable trip to Disney World. He credited the AI with making savings fun and achievable.

Case Study 3: Small Business Success

A bakery in New York faced challenges managing its budget due to fluctuating ingredient prices and seasonal demand. The owner decided to implement an AI-powered financial management tool.

Inventory and Cost Analysis

The AI analyzed historical sales data and supplier invoices. It identified:

- Ingredients that were consistently overpriced compared to market trends.
- Wasted inventory that could be reduced by adjusting order quantities.

Optimized Spending

The AI suggested:

- Switching to suppliers with better pricing.
- Reducing orders for low-demand items.

Allocating more budget toward high-performing products like cupcakes and artisan bread.

Dynamic Budget Adjustments

As the bakery's revenue varied seasonally, the AI adapted the budget to match. During slower months, it reduced spending on non-essential items, such as decorations and marketing. During peak seasons, it is recommended to invest more in staffing and advertising.

The bakery increased its profit margins by 15% within six months. The owner noted, "The AI gave us clarity we never had before. It felt like having a financial analyst on our team."

Case Study 4: Emily's College Savings Plan

Emily, a single mother, was determined to save for her son's college education. However, managing monthly expenses while building a savings fund seemed overwhelming. She turned to an AI-driven budgeting platform for guidance.

Income and Expense Breakdown

The AI analyzed Emily's income and categorized her expenses. It identified areas where she could cut costs:

- Reduced spending on entertainment.

- Lowered energy bills by suggesting energy-efficient practices.

Goal-Oriented Savings

The platform enabled her to set a specific goal: saving $50,000 over 10 years. It then calculated:

- The monthly amount she needed to save.
- Adjustments would be made if unexpected expenses arose.

Investment Advice

The AI suggested low-risk investment options to grow her savings faster. It provided easy-to-understand explanations about the benefits of compound interest and recommended periodic reviews of her progress.

Impact

After three years, Emily had already saved $20,000, exceeding her initial expectations. She remarked, "The AI made the impossible feel doable."

Case Study 5: A Freelancer's Financial Stability

Mark, a freelance graphic designer, struggled with inconsistent income. His earnings fluctuated monthly, making it hard to create a stable budget. He adopted an AI-driven budgeting tool designed for freelancers.

Predicting Income Trends

The AI used historical data to predict his average monthly income and identify peak earning periods. This helped Mark understand when he could save more aggressively and when to be cautious with spending.

Expense Prioritization

The AI categorized his expenses into:

- Fixed costs like rent and utilities.
- Variable costs, such as dining out and entertainment.

Suggested cutting down on non-essential expenses during low-income months.

Building a Safety Net

The tool helped Mark build an emergency fund by automatically transferring a percentage of his income during high-earning months. It also provided insights into managing taxes efficiently as a freelancer.

Outcome

Mark achieved financial stability within a year. He shared, "The AI taught me how to manage uncertainty and gave me confidence in my finances."

Case Study 6: A University's Financial Revamp

A mid-sized university was facing budget deficits due to poor expense management and declining enrollment. The administration decided to adopt AI-driven budgeting software to address these challenges.

Expense Analysis

The AI reviewed the university's financial records and identified unnecessary spending:

- Overlapping software licenses.
- Inefficient energy use in older buildings.

Resource Allocation

The AI provided recommendations to reallocate resources:

Invest in digital marketing to attract more students.

Reduce costs by centralizing procurement processes.

Adaptive Budget Planning

The system created dynamic budgets that adjusted to changes in enrollment numbers and external funding.

Outcome

Within two years, the university achieved a balanced budget and saw a 10% increase in enrollment. The administration praised the AI for its detailed insights and actionable strategies.

These case studies illustrate the diverse ways in which Generative AI is revolutionizing budgeting. From individuals overcoming personal financial challenges to businesses achieving operational efficiency, AI-driven tools offer solutions that are adaptable, precise, and impactful. As more people embrace these technologies, budgeting will continue to evolve into a dynamic, data-driven process, empowering users to achieve their financial goals with confidence.

CHAPTER 3

INVESTING SMARTER

Investing has always been about making informed decisions to grow wealth while managing risks. The arrival of Generative AI is transforming how we approach investments, providing tools that not only analyze data but also generate innovative strategies. This chapter examines how Generative AI enhances investment decisions, optimizes portfolio management, and facilitates ethical investing in a manner that is straightforward, efficient, and forward-thinking.

AI-DRIVEN INVESTMENT STRATEGIES AND MARKET ANALYSIS

Generative AI simplifies the process of analyzing markets. Traditionally, investors rely on historical data and trends to inform their decisions. However, Generative AI goes a step further—it not only interprets historical data but also predicts future trends and generates strategies that adapt to different market conditions. Here's how it works:

1. **Predicting Market Trends:** Generative AI uses advanced algorithms to study patterns in financial markets. It examines how stocks, commodities, or other investments performed under similar conditions in the past. By doing so, it predicts potential outcomes, giving investors an edge. For example, if certain stocks are likely to rise based on historical patterns and current economic conditions, the AI highlights these opportunities early.

Investors can use this insight to make proactive decisions, avoiding the common pitfalls of reactive investing.

2. **Simulating Market Scenarios:** One unique ability of Generative AI is the creation of simulations for various market situations. These simulations show how an investment might perform under different conditions, such as an economic slowdown or a sudden surge in demand for a product. By running these scenarios, investors can test their strategies without taking actual risks. For example, A company planning to invest in renewable energy can use AI simulations to see how policy changes or technological breakthroughs might impact the industry.

3. **Spotting Hidden Opportunities:** Markets are vast, and it's easy for even experienced investors to miss out on opportunities. Generative AI excels in processing enormous amounts of data quickly, identifying trends and investments that human analysts might overlook. This could mean spotting an undervalued stock or identifying a niche market with high growth potential.

THE ROLE OF ROBO-ADVISORS IN PERSONALIZED PORTFOLIO MANAGEMENT

Managing investments can be intimidating, especially for those who are new to the process. Robo-advisors, powered by Generative AI, are simplifying this by automating portfolio management and offering personalized investment solutions.

1. What Are Robo-Advisors?

Robo-advisors are digital tools that manage your investments for you. They ask fundamental questions about your financial goals, risk tolerance, and timeline, then use AI to create a portfolio tailored specifically for you. With Generative AI, these advisors have become smarter, providing solutions that are not only customized but also dynamic.

2. How Do Robo-Advisors Work?

- Data Collection: They gather information about your financial status and objectives.
- Portfolio Generation: Using Generative AI, they create a portfolio optimized for your goals, whether it's saving for retirement or growing wealth over the short term.
- Continuous Adjustment: Unlike traditional advisors, robo-advisors monitor your investments constantly, making adjustments as needed. If the market changes (Pooya Azadi, 2024; Mousa Al-Kfairy, 2024), your goals shift and adapt accordingly.

3. Advantages of Robo-Advisors

- Cost-Effective: Robo-advisors are generally more affordable than traditional financial advisors, making them accessible to a broader audience.
- Convenience: Once set up, they require minimal input, saving you time and effort.
- Consistency: Generative AI eliminates emotional bias,

ensuring that decisions are based on data and logic rather than fear or greed.

4. Real-Life Example

Imagine someone just starting their career with limited savings but a strong desire to invest. A robo-advisor can create a diversified portfolio, track it over time, and adjust it based on performance, all without requiring the individual to possess expert market knowledge.

ETHICAL INVESTING SUPPORTED BY GENERATIVE AI

As awareness of social and environmental issues grows, more people are looking to invest in ways that align with their values. Ethical investing involves selecting investments that align with personal or societal principles, such as sustainability, fairness, and social responsibility. Generative AI plays a crucial role in making this process easier and more effective.

Ethical investing prioritizes companies or industries that meet specific moral or environmental standards. For example, it may focus on:

- Renewable energy companies instead of fossil fuels.
- Organizations that promote diversity and inclusion.
- Businesses with strong environmental, social, and governance (ESG) practices.

Challenges in Ethical Investing

Ethical investing isn't always straightforward. Investors may struggle to identify companies that genuinely meet their values, especially when some businesses engage in "greenwashing" or misleading practices. This is where Generative AI steps in.

HOW GENERATIVE AI ENHANCES ETHICAL INVESTING

Identifying ESG Leaders: Generative AI can analyze large datasets, including financial reports, media coverage, and public statements, to evaluate companies' ESG performance. It ensures that only genuinely responsible companies are included in an ethical portfolio.

Balancing Returns with Ethics: One concern with ethical investing is whether it compromises financial performance. Generative AI generates investment strategies that maximize returns while adhering to ethical principles.

Avoiding Greenwashing: By examining detailed data, AI can spot discrepancies between a company's claims and its actual practices, helping investors avoid misleading investments.

Practical Applications

Imagine a fund focused on combating climate change. Generative AI could help build this fund by:

- Selecting companies that are actively reducing their carbon footprint.

- Simulating the long-term impact of these companies on the environment.
- Monitoring their performance to ensure they continue meeting sustainability goals.

REAL-WORLD EXAMPLES OF GENERATIVE AI IN INVESTMENT

Case Study 1: Enhancing Portfolio Diversification

A multinational investment firm uses Generative AI to create highly diversified portfolios. By analyzing thousands of data points, the AI ensures that portfolios are spread across industries and regions, reducing risk while maximizing potential gains.

Case Study 2: Ethical Investment Growth

A socially responsible investment fund employed Generative AI to identify top-performing ESG companies. Over the course of three years, the fund outperformed traditional indices by focusing on companies with strong ethical practices.

Case Study 3: Retirement Planning Made Simple

An individual nearing retirement used a Generative AI-powered robo-advisor to manage her savings. The AI created a low-risk, high-yield portfolio that adapted to her changing needs as she transitioned into retirement.

THE FUTURE OF GENERATIVE AI IN INVESTING

Generative AI is not just a tool for the present; it's shaping the future of investing. As models become more advanced, we can expect:

- Greater Accessibility: Investment tools powered by AI will become even more user-friendly, making them accessible to people of all income levels.
- Improved Accuracy: As Generative AI continues to learn, its predictions and strategies will become even more precise.
- Global Reach: AI-powered tools will allow investors to explore opportunities across borders, breaking down barriers to international investment.

AI-Driven Investment Strategies and Market Analysis

Generative AI has ushered in a new era in investment strategies and market analysis, providing tools that revolutionize decision-making in the financial world. With its ability to analyze vast amounts of data, predict trends, and simulate various scenarios, Generative AI enables investors to make smarter, more informed decisions. This section explains how Generative AI drives investment strategies and market analysis in simple, clear terms.

Understanding AI-Driven Investment Strategies

Investing involves putting money into financial opportunities with the hope of gaining a profit. Traditionally, investment decisions were based on historical data, expert advice, and intuition. However, Generative AI has transformed this process by introducing advanced predictive capabilities and dynamic decision-making tools.

1. Generative AI's Role in Decision-Making

Generative AI uses algorithms trained on historical financial data to predict market movements and recommend strategies. Unlike older tools, Generative AI doesn't just rely on past patterns; it generates new possibilities, allowing investors to explore innovative strategies.

Example: Imagine an investor trying to decide which stocks to buy. Generative AI analyzes millions of data points, including past stock performance, market news, and global economic trends, to suggest which stocks have the best growth potential.

2. Advanced Predictive Analysis

Generative AI excels at identifying patterns in financial data. By analyzing past market behavior and current trends, it can forecast future changes with a high degree of accuracy. Scenario Forecasting: AI models simulate various economic conditions, such as a rise in interest rates or an oil price shock, to illustrate how these changes may impact investments. This allows investors to prepare for potential outcomes before they happen.

3. Risk Assessment and Diversification

One key to successful investing is managing risk. Generative AI assesses potential risks by analyzing factors such as market volatility and historical performance. It helps investors diversify their portfolios, ensuring that their investments are spread across different asset classes, industries, or geographic regions. Diversification minimizes the impact of losses in one area by balancing them with gains in others. Generative AI makes this process easier and more precise.

The Process of Market Analysis Using Generative AI

Market analysis involves understanding how financial markets behave to make informed investment decisions. Generative AI enhances this process in several ways:

1. Real-Time Data Processing

Financial markets are dynamic, with prices changing constantly. Generative AI can process real-time data from stock exchanges, economic reports, and social media, providing investors with instant insights.

Example: If a major company announces a new product, AI can analyze the news and predict how the company's stock price might respond, allowing investors to act quickly.

2. Identifying Market Trends

Generative AI identifies long-term trends that are not immediately visible to human analysts. For example, it might detect an emerging interest in renewable energy investments before it becomes widely recognized, giving investors a head start.

Example: AI might highlight how electric vehicle stocks are likely to grow based on global policies encouraging green energy.

3. Behavioral Analysis

Generative AI also considers the impact of human behavior on markets. It studies patterns like panic selling during market crashes or overbuying during booms. This behavioral insight helps investors avoid making emotionally driven decisions.

PRACTICAL APPLICATIONS OF GENERATIVE AI IN INVESTMENT STRATEGIES

The practical uses of Generative AI in investing are vast. It assists in creating personalized strategies, performing detailed analyses, and offering recommendations that adapt to individual goals.

1. Portfolio Optimization

Generative AI helps investors optimize their portfolios by balancing risk and reward. It evaluates which assets to include in a portfolio and determines their ideal proportions based on an investor's goals and objectives.

Example: An investor aiming for steady income might be guided toward bonds and dividend-paying stocks, while someone seeking high growth could focus on tech startups.

2. Scenario Testing and Stress Analysis

One of the most powerful features of Generative AI is its ability to simulate various market conditions.

Stress Testing: It tests how an investment portfolio would perform under extreme scenarios, such as a financial crisis or a sudden drop in oil prices.

Benefit: This enables investors to identify weaknesses in their strategies and make adjustments to enhance resilience.

3. Intelligent Alerts

Generative AI systems can monitor the market and send alerts when opportunities or risks arise.

Example: If the stock price of a company suddenly drops due to temporary bad news, AI might notify an investor that it's a good buying opportunity.

How Generative AI Improves Investment Outcomes

Generative AI enhances investment results by improving accuracy, saving time, and enabling smarter decisions.

1. Improved Accuracy

By analyzing more data and performing deeper calculations, Generative AI reduces errors in predictions. This level of precision enables investors to avoid poor choices and maximize their returns.

2. Faster Decision-Making

The speed at which Generative AI processes data is unmatched. Investors no longer have to spend hours analyzing reports or reading market news; AI does this in seconds, allowing quicker decisions.

3. Customization and Personalization

Generative AI adapts its strategies based on an investor's preferences. For instance, it can focus on ethical investing for someone who values sustainability or prioritize high-growth opportunities for a risk-tolerant individual.

Ethical Implications of AI-Driven Investments

Although Generative AI offers many benefits, it's important to consider ethical aspects when using it for investments.

Avoiding Market Manipulation

Generative AI must be used responsibly to prevent exploitation of market loopholes or unethical trading practices.

Ensuring Fair Access

Advanced AI tools should be accessible to a wide range of investors, not just large financial institutions. This ensures a more level playing field in the market.

Transparency in Decision-Making

Generative AI models must be transparent about how they arrive at predictions or recommendations. This helps investors trust the technology and make informed decisions.

CASE STUDY: GENERATIVE AI IN ACTION

Scenario: Predicting Market Opportunities

A global investment firm implemented a Generative AI tool to analyze data from multiple sources, including stock market trends, economic indicators, and news articles. The AI detected an early trend in the adoption of renewable energy stocks, prompting the firm to invest heavily in this sector. Over the course of three years, these investments yielded a return 20% higher than the market average.

Limitations and Challenges

While Generative AI is a game-changer, it is not without limitations.

- Data Dependency: Generative AI requires large, high-quality datasets. Poor data can lead to inaccurate predictions.
- Complexity: Some investors may find it challenging to comprehend the outputs of AI tools, which can make them hesitant to fully rely on the technology.
- Ethical Risks: As mentioned earlier, there is a risk of bias in AI models if they are trained on biased data.

The Role of Robo-Advisors in Personalized Portfolio Management

The investment world has undergone a seismic shift with the

advent of robo-advisors. Powered by the advanced capabilities of Generative AI, these digital platforms are revolutionizing the management of portfolios, offering a level of precision, personalization, and accessibility that was once unimaginable. Let's dive deeper into what robo-advisors are, how they operate, and the immense value they bring to personalized portfolio management.

What Are Robo-Advisors?

Robo-advisors are automated platforms that use AI algorithms to create and manage investment portfolios. Unlike traditional financial advisors, they rely on data-driven decision-making to provide tailored solutions for individual investors. These systems have gained popularity because of their ability to simplify investment processes and make personalized financial planning more accessible to a broader audience.

At the core of a robo-advisor is Generative AI, which continuously learns from market trends and individual investor preferences. This AI-driven learning enables the platform to adapt and refine its recommendations, ensuring that each portfolio aligns with the user's financial goals and risk tolerance.

How Robo-Advisors Work

The journey of using a robo-advisor begins with understanding the investor. Users typically start by answering a series of questions about their financial goals, risk tolerance, and investment horizon. For example, a young professional looking to save for retirement in 30 years will have a different portfolio from a retiree seeking steady income.

After gathering this input, the robo-advisor uses Generative AI to analyze the data and design a personalized portfolio. The platform identifies the best combination of assets, such as stocks, bonds, or ETFs, to meet the user's goals. It considers various factors, including market trends, historical performance, and risk diversification, to create an optimized strategy.

One of the key strengths of robo-advisors is their ability to monitor portfolios in real-time. Unlike traditional advisors, who may conduct periodic reviews, robo-advisors continuously track market conditions and portfolio performance. If a significant market change occurs, the platform can automatically rebalance the portfolio, ensuring that it remains aligned with the investor's objectives.

Personalization at Scale

Generative AI allows robo-advisors to offer a highly personalized experience to millions of users simultaneously. Each portfolio is unique, reflecting the specific needs and preferences of the individual investor. This scalability is a game-changer, making expert financial management accessible to people who might not have been able to afford traditional advisory services.

For instance, a person saving for a home in five years might be advised to prioritize low-risk investments, while someone planning for long-term wealth accumulation might be guided toward a diversified mix of higher-risk assets. Generative AI ensures that each recommendation is based on comprehensive data analysis, tailored to the user's financial journey.

Cost Efficiency

One of the most attractive features of robo-advisors is their cost efficiency. Traditional financial advisors often charge high fees, which can eat into investment returns over time. In contrast, robo-advisors operate on significantly lower costs, making them an appealing choice for both new and experienced investors.

The reduced fees are possible because robo-advisors automate many of the processes that traditional advisors handle manually. From analyzing market data to executing trades, these platforms streamline operations, passing the cost savings on to the user. This affordability has democratized access to high-quality investment management, enabling individuals with smaller portfolios to benefit from professional guidance.

Continuous Monitoring and Rebalancing

Robo-advisors excel in their ability to monitor portfolios around the clock. Markets are dynamic, with constant fluctuations influenced by global events, economic trends, and investor sentiment. For human advisors, keeping up with these changes can be challenging. Robo-advisors, however, thrive in this environment.

Generative AI ensures that the platform continually analyzes the latest data. If a portfolio drifts away from its intended allocation, perhaps because stocks in one sector have outperformed, robo-advisors automatically rebalance the investments. This process involves selling overperforming assets and reallocating funds to underperforming ones, maintaining the desired risk-reward balance.

This automated rebalancing is not only efficient but also removes the emotional biases that often lead individual investors to make suboptimal decisions. For instance, an investor might hesitate to sell a stock that has performed well, fearing they might miss out on further gains. Robo-advisors make these decisions objectively, guided by data rather than emotion.

Accessibility and User-Friendliness

Robo-advisors are designed to be user-friendly, catering to individuals with little to no prior investment experience. The onboarding process is straightforward, with intuitive interfaces that guide users through every step. Most platforms provide clear explanations of their recommendations, helping users understand why certain investments are chosen.

This accessibility extends to the types of investors who can use robo-advisors. Whether you are a college student starting your first investment account or a seasoned professional managing a substantial portfolio, robo-advisors can adapt to your needs. This inclusivity has made them a popular choice across diverse demographic groups.

Tax Optimization

Another significant advantage of robo-advisors is their ability to optimize investments for tax efficiency. Generative AI algorithms analyze an investor's taxable and tax-advantaged accounts, strategically placing investments to minimize tax liabilities. For instance, high-yield bonds might be allocated to a tax-advantaged retirement account, while stocks with long-term growth potential could be placed in a taxable account to take advantage of lower capital gains rates.

Some robo-advisors also offer tax-loss harvesting, a strategy that involves selling underperforming assets to offset taxable gains. This feature, traditionally reserved for high-net-worth individuals with access to specialized advisors, is now available to everyday investors through Generative AI-powered platforms.

HYBRID MODELS: COMBINING HUMAN AND AI EXPERTISE

While robo-advisors excel in automation and efficiency, some investors prefer a human touch. Hybrid models, which combine

Generative AI with human financial advisors, offer the best of both worlds. In these models, Generative AI handles routine tasks like portfolio analysis and rebalancing, while human advisors provide personalized guidance for complex decisions.

For instance, an investor navigating a significant life event, such as selling a business or planning a major inheritance, might benefit from the expertise of a human advisor. The combination of AI's precision and a human's emotional intelligence ensures that these unique needs are addressed effectively.

Success Stories

The real-world impact of robo-advisors is evident in numerous success stories. Consider a young couple saving for their first home. By using a robo-advisor, they were able to create a low-risk, goal-oriented portfolio. The platform automatically adjusted their investments as their savings grew, ensuring that they remained on track to meet their goal within five years.

Another example is a retiree seeking steady income from their investments. A Generative AI-powered robo-advisor analyzed their expenses, risk tolerance, and market conditions to create a portfolio that provided regular income while preserving capital. The retiree could enjoy peace of mind, knowing their investments were being managed with precision.

Overcoming Limitations

While robo-advisors offer numerous advantages, they are not without limitations. Some critics argue that these platforms lack the nuanced understanding that a human advisor provides. For example, a robo-advisor might not fully grasp the emotional significance of an investor's attachment to a particular asset.

However, advancements in Generative AI are continuously bridging these gaps. By incorporating sentiment analysis and other advanced techniques, robo-advisors are becoming increasingly adept at understanding and catering to the unique needs of individual investors.

The Future of Robo-Advisors

The evolution of robo-advisors is closely tied to the advancements in Generative AI. As technology continues to improve, these platforms are expected to become even more sophisticated. Future developments may include enhanced predictive capabilities, deeper personalization, and greater integration with other financial tools.

For investors, this means a future where financial management is not only more accessible but also more empowering. Robo-advisors will continue to democratize investment opportunities, helping individuals achieve their financial goals with confidence and ease.

Detecting Greenwashing

Greenwashing, where companies exaggerate or falsely claim their environmental or social achievements, is a significant challenge in ethical investing. Generative AI can help cut through the noise by cross-referencing corporate claims with independent data sources, such as third-party audits or news reports, thereby providing a more accurate representation of the facts. By detecting inconsistencies, AI ensures that deceptive marketing strategies do not mislead investors, identifying

Emerging Ethical Trends

Ethical considerations are not static—they evolve as societal values change. Generative AI is adept at identifying emerging trends in consumer behavior, regulatory developments, or cultural shifts that might affect investment opportunities. For instance, it could highlight the growing importance of renewable energy or the increasing demand for companies to adopt diversity and inclusion policies. This forward-looking capability helps investors stay ahead of the curve.

Balancing Ethics with Financial Performance

A common concern for ethical investors is whether prioritizing values might come at the cost of financial returns. Generative AI addresses this concern by generating optimized portfolios that balance ethical criteria with strong performance potential.

By simulating various market scenarios, AI ensures that portfolios remain resilient while adhering to ethical principles.

For instance, an investor may want to support clean energy but be concerned about the volatility of renewable energy stocks. Generative AI can design a diversified portfolio that includes stable, ethically aligned investments to offset this risk. This approach ensures that ethical investing does not compromise financial security.

Building Diverse and Inclusive Portfolios

Generative AI also supports diversity and inclusion within portfolios. By analyzing data on corporate governance, workforce demographics, and community impact, AI can identify companies that actively promote equality and inclusion. These businesses often demonstrate strong long-term potential, as they attract talent, foster innovation, and build positive reputations.

For example, an AI tool might flag a tech company that prioritizes hiring women and underrepresented groups in leadership positions. Including such companies in a portfolio not only aligns with ethical values but also supports a broader societal push toward fairness and equity.

Empowering Individual Investors

Ethical investing is no longer limited to large institutions or wealthy individuals. Generative AI has democratized access to ethical investment opportunities, empowering everyday investors to align their money with their values. AI-powered robo-advisors, for instance, can help individuals identify ethical funds, set goals, and track their impact over time. These tools simplify the process, making ethical investing accessible to anyone with an internet connection.

An example of this is an AI-driven app that allows users to exclude specific industries, such as fossil fuels or tobacco, from their portfolios. The app then generates a list of alternative investments that align with the user's preferences. This level of customization ensures that ethical investing is both personal and impactful.

Generating New Opportunities in Ethical Investing

Generative AI goes beyond analyzing existing data—it can create entirely new investment opportunities. For example, AI might identify an untapped market for green technologies in developing countries or forecast the rise of sustainable fashion brands. These insights allow investors to support innovative solutions to global challenges, often before they become mainstream.

This proactive approach not only drives positive change but also positions investors to benefit from early-stage growth in emerging industries. By identifying where capital can have the most significant impact, Generative AI transforms ethical investing from a reactive process into a forward-looking strategy.

Addressing Challenges in Ethical Investing

While Generative AI offers numerous benefits, ethical investing still faces challenges that must be addressed. For example, ethical priorities vary significantly among individuals, making it challenging to establish a universal standard. What one investor views as ethical might not align with another's values. Generative AI can help navigate this complexity by tailoring recommendations to each investor's unique criteria.

Another challenge is the lack of standardized reporting on ESG metrics. While many companies now provide sustainability reports, the quality and consistency of these disclosures can vary. Generative AI can bridge this gap by aggregating and analyzing data from multiple sources, ensuring a more comprehensive understanding of a company's ethical impact.

Generative AI's Role in Shaping the Future of Ethical Investing

As Generative AI continues to evolve, its potential to transform ethical investing grows. Future advancements could include:

- Real-time tracking of a company's ethical performance, providing investors with continuous updates.
- Enhanced predictive models that anticipate the long-term impact of specific investments on society and the environment.
- Greater integration with global sustainability initiatives, aligning

investments with international goals such as the United Nations Sustainable Development Goals (SDGs).

These innovations will not only make ethical investing more effective but also expand its reach, enabling more people to participate in building a better world.

Case Study: Supporting Ethical Investment Funds

Generative AI has demonstrated its transformative potential in ethical investing through its application in the creation of targeted ethical investment funds. A notable example comes from a leading financial institution that set out to design a fund centered around renewable energy and sustainable agriculture. This initiative aimed to merge financial profitability with social responsibility, appealing to a growing segment of investors prioritizing ethical considerations.

The process began with the deployment of Generative AI models trained to analyze extensive datasets. These datasets included market performance indicators, Environmental, Social, and Governance (ESG) metrics, and reports from regulatory bodies. The AI identified trends that human analysts might overlook, such as the rapid adoption of solar energy in specific regions or the emergence of innovative, sustainable farming technologies. By synthesizing this data, the AI was able to pinpoint companies that not only had a positive ethical impact but also demonstrated strong financial potential.

One of the key strengths of Generative AI in this context was its ability to cross-reference ESG claims with external, independent sources. For example, while a company might report a reduction in carbon emissions, the AI validated this claim against government environmental audits and third-party certifications. This verification process minimized the risk of greenwashing and ensured that only genuinely sustainable companies were included in the fund.

As the fund took shape, the AI played an integral role in optimizing the portfolio. It simulated thousands of market scenarios to assess how different combinations of assets would perform under varying economic conditions. This rigorous testing enabled the financial institution to develop a robust portfolio that strikes a balance between ethical priorities and financial resilience.

Within three years, the fund achieved remarkable success, consistently outperforming traditional investment funds. This was attributed to several factors:

- Alignment with Emerging Trends: The focus on renewable energy and sustainable agriculture aligned with global shifts toward sustainability, attracting both institutional and individual investors.
- Resilience in Market Downturns: The AI-designed portfolio demonstrated strong performance even during economic downturns, as it included companies with stable, future-proof

business models.

- Investor Confidence: The transparency provided by Generative AI, including detailed reports on the ethical and financial impact of each investment, built trust among investors who were initially skeptical about ethical funds.

Moreover, the success of this fund had a ripple effect on the broader investment landscape. Inspired by this case, other financial institutions began exploring the use of Generative AI to create similar funds, further advancing the integration of ethics and profitability in finance. This case underscores how Generative AI can bridge the gap between values-driven investing and the practical demands of achieving strong returns, offering a model for the future of ethical investing.

Generative AI has revolutionized ethical investing by providing tools to analyze, predict, and create opportunities that align with personal and societal values. It ensures transparency, combats challenges like greenwashing, and empowers investors to make decisions that benefit both their finances and the world around them. As technology advances, the synergy between ethical investing and Generative AI will only deepen, paving the way for a future where doing good and doing well are the same.

CHAPTER 4

ENHANCING SAVINGS

Saving money is a critical part of managing personal and business finances. It's what helps us prepare for emergencies, achieve life goals, and secure our futures. With the rise of Generative AI, saving has become more effective and easier to manage. Generative AI uses advanced technology to predict financial needs, automate saving processes, and personalize strategies to suit individual goals. This chapter explores how Generative AI enhances savings through predictive planning, automation, and real-world success stories.

HOW PREDICTIVE SAVINGS PLANS WORK

Predictive savings plans use Generative AI to analyze past financial behavior and forecast future needs. These tools take the guesswork out of saving by showing exactly how much to save, when to save, and where to save it.

1. **Understanding Spending Habits**

   Generative AI tools start by examining spending patterns. For example, they identify how much you typically spend on necessities like rent and groceries versus non-essentials like entertainment or dining out.

   AI tools can flag areas where spending can be reduced without drastically impacting your lifestyle. By understanding your unique spending habits, Generative AI ensures savings plans are practical and achievable.

2. Setting Clear Goals

A good savings plan starts with clear, measurable goals. Generative AI tools help define these goals based on your financial situation and aspirations:

- Short-term goals: Examples include saving for a vacation, an upcoming celebration, or an emergency fund.
- Long-term goals: These could involve retirement, buying a home, or funding your child's education.

AI ensures these goals are realistic by aligning them with your income and expenses. For instance, if you want to save $10,000 in two years, AI calculates how much you need to save each month and adjusts for unexpected changes.

3. Adapting to Changes

One of the most valuable features of Generative AI is its ability to adapt in real-time. Unlike traditional savings plans, which are fixed, AI-powered plans adjust to life's changes:

- Sudden expenses: If a car repair or medical bill disrupts your budget, AI can recommend scaling back on non-essential expenses temporarily.
- Income changes: Whether you get a raise or lose a source of income, AI recalibrates your savings plan to keep you on track.

This flexibility makes it easier to stick to savings goals even when life doesn't go as planned.

AUTOMATING SAVINGS FOR SIMPLICITY

Automation streamlines the process of saving. Generative AI can manage savings on your behalf, ensuring that funds are set aside consistently without requiring constant attention.

Automatic Transfers

One of the simplest ways AI automates savings is by setting up regular transfers from your checking account to your savings account:

- Fixed contributions: You can choose to transfer a set amount monthly, ensuring steady progress toward your goals.
- Dynamic contributions: AI tools can adjust the transfer amount based on your cash flow. For instance, during months when you spend less, the tool might allocate more to savings.

By automating transfers, you don't have to rely on willpower to save. It happens automatically

ENHANCING SAVINGS

Saving money is an essential part of financial health, but many people find it challenging to save consistently. Generative AI has introduced innovative ways to simplify the process, helping individuals and families save more effectively by predicting future needs, automating savings, and adapting to financial changes. This chapter explores how Generative AI transforms savings through predictive plans, automated tools, and real-life success stories.

Predictive Savings Plans

Generative AI excels in predicting future trends and providing insights that can help you save more strategically. These savings plans rely on analyzing your financial data—like income, expenses, and spending habits—to anticipate your needs and goals. The ability of Generative AI to adapt its recommendations in real-time makes it a reliable tool for both short- and long-term planning.

For instance, if you're saving for a major life event, such as buying a house or sending your child to college, Generative AI can estimate how much you'll need and when. By analyzing inflation trends, housing market conditions, or tuition fee increases, it can provide a roadmap to meet your target. This type of guidance helps you feel confident that you're saving the right amount at the right time.

Another strength of Generative AI is its ability to dynamically adjust savings recommendations. If your financial situation changes, such as an increase in income or an unexpected expense, the AI can instantly recalculate your plan to keep you on track. This adaptability ensures that your savings remain aligned with your goals without requiring constant manual adjustments.

Automating Savings Based on Behavior and Goals

One of the most powerful applications of Generative AI in savings is automation. By removing the burden of manual effort, automated tools ensure that saving becomes a consistent and stress-free process. Generative AI can analyze your spending patterns and income flow to determine the best times and amounts to save, making the process effortless and reliable.

For example, many people struggle with setting aside money because it feels restrictive. Generative AI addresses this challenge by learning your financial behavior and identifying opportunities to save without significantly impacting your lifestyle. If you spend less during certain months, the AI may allocate more savings during those periods. Conversely, if it detects that you're overspending, it might suggest smaller, manageable contributions to keep you on track without creating financial strain.

AI-powered savings tools also incorporate features like "round-up" savings, where small amounts from everyday transactions are automatically moved into a savings account. For instance, if you buy a coffee for $3.75, the AI rounds it up to $4.00 and saves the extra $0.25. Over time, these small contributions can accumulate, forming a steady savings habit with minimal effort.

Another way Generative AI automates savings is by categorizing your income and allocating a portion to savings as soon as you receive your payment. This method, often referred to as "paying yourself first," ensures that saving becomes a priority rather than an afterthought. By analyzing your financial goals, the AI can suggest the most suitable account types for your savings, such as high-yield accounts or certificates of deposit (CDs), which offer higher returns.

Personalized Savings Recommendations

One of the standout features of Generative AI is its ability to personalize savings strategies. Everyone's financial situation is unique, and a one-size-fits-all approach rarely works. Generative AI takes into account your circumstances, such as your income level, spending habits, and future goals, to create a tailored savings plan.

For instance, if you're saving for a vacation, the AI might calculate how much you need to set aside each month to reach your goal by the desired date. If you're working toward retirement, it can forecast how much you'll need based on factors like inflation and expected lifestyle costs. These personalized recommendations take the guesswork out of saving, making it easier to stay motivated and focused.

The adaptability of Generative AI also ensures that your savings strategy evolves with your life. If you receive a raise or experience a drop in income, the AI recalibrates your plan to match your new reality. This flexibility is particularly valuable in times of economic uncertainty, where staying on top of your finances is crucial.

Real-Life Success Stories

The impact of Generative AI on savings becomes even more evident when examining real-world examples. These stories demonstrate how individuals and families have leveraged AI to overcome financial challenges and achieve their objectives.

One inspiring case involves a young professional named Emma. Emma struggled to save consistently due to fluctuating expenses and a lack of financial discipline. By using a Generative AI-powered app, she was able to analyze her spending habits and identify areas where she could cut back. The AI automated her savings by setting aside small amounts after each paycheck. Within two years, Emma saved enough for a down payment on her first home, a goal she previously thought was out of reach.

Another example is a family of four working to save for their children's education. They used an AI-driven savings tool that calculated future tuition costs and created a step-by-step plan to meet those expenses. The AI adjusted their contributions based on monthly cash flow, ensuring that they could save without compromising their daily needs. By the time their eldest child was ready for college, the family had surpassed their savings goal.

Small business owners have also benefited from Generative AI. Take the case of a retail shop owner who struggled with cash flow management. By leveraging an AI tool, the owner was able to identify seasonal trends and allocate a portion of peak-season profits to a savings account. This strategy enabled the business to establish a financial cushion that proved invaluable during an unexpected economic downturn.

Generative AI and the Future of Savings

The integration of Generative AI into savings tools is not just a technological advancement; it's a transformative shift in how we approach financial management. By combining predictive analytics with automation and personalization, Generative AI offers a comprehensive solution to the challenges of saving. It empowers individuals to make more informed financial decisions, enabling them to achieve their goals with greater confidence.

As technology continues to evolve, the capabilities of Generative AI will only grow. Future savings tools may include even more advanced features, such as real-time collaboration with financial advisors or integration with broader financial ecosystems. These developments will make saving even more accessible and effective for people from all walks of life.

Generative AI provides a roadmap for more effective and efficient saving. By predicting future needs, automating contributions, and personalizing strategies, it eliminates many of the traditional barriers to saving. Whether you're building an emergency fund, planning for a major purchase, or securing your financial future, Generative AI is a valuable partner in your journey toward financial stability.

PREDICTIVE SAVINGS PLANS: UNLOCKING THE POWER OF GENERATIVE AI FOR YOUR FUTURE

Saving money is a fundamental part of financial security, yet it often feels daunting. The advent of Generative AI offers a solution that transforms traditional savings methods into dynamic, data-driven strategies. Predictive savings plans, powered by Generative AI, provide individuals and businesses with a way to anticipate financial needs, optimize contributions, and adapt to changing circumstances effortlessly. Let's explore how this cutting-edge technology is reshaping the art of saving money.

Predictive Savings Plans?

At its core, a predictive savings plan utilizes advanced AI algorithms to forecast your future financial needs and create a personalized savings strategy tailored to you. Unlike static plans that rely on fixed contributions, these plans are dynamic in nature. They continuously analyze data, such as your income, spending habits, and lifestyle changes, to ensure you're always on track to meet your goals.

For example, imagine you're saving for a major life event like buying a house. Traditional methods might suggest setting aside a fixed amount each month. Generative AI, on the other hand, goes beyond this by analyzing market trends, inflation rates, and your financial behavior to predict how much you'll need and adjust your savings plan in real time.

The Role of Generative AI in Forecasting Needs

Generative AI excels at identifying patterns in large sets of data. When applied to savings, it examines factors such as past spending habits, recurring expenses, and future financial events, including retirement or tuition payments. This predictive capability empowers you to make informed decisions, minimizing the guesswork.

Imagine a young professional planning for retirement. Generative AI can assess their current income, estimate their future earning potential, and project the cost-of-living decades down the line. By doing so, it provides a clear savings target and recommends the optimal pace to reach it.

Additionally, this technology adapts to changes in life. If someone switches jobs, receives a raise, or encounters unexpected expenses, the savings plan recalibrates to ensure it remains relevant and effective.

Adapting to Life's Uncertainties

One of the most impressive features of predictive savings plans is their ability to handle uncertainties. Life rarely goes as planned—unexpected medical bills, job changes, or economic shifts can derail even the best financial strategies. Generative AI shines in these moments by reassessing your financial situation and suggesting adjustments to keep your savings on track.

For example, if a family experiences a sudden increase in expenses, such as higher energy bills during the winter, the AI can identify discretionary spending areas to reduce, ensuring savings contributions continue without significant disruption in the short term. This level of adaptability offers peace of mind, knowing your plan is prepared to weather life's ups and downs.

Customizing Plans for Individual Goals

No two people have identical financial needs, and Generative AI recognizes this. Predictive savings plans are highly personalized, considering a wide range of factors unique to each user. These factors include:

- Monthly income and expenses.
- Long-term financial goals, such as homeownership or retirement.
- Short-term objectives, like saving for a vacation or an emergency fund.
- Lifestyle choices and preferences.

For instance, someone planning an international trip within the next year might receive recommendations to set aside a specific amount each month. Meanwhile, a parent saving for a child's education could benefit from a more gradual plan that takes inflation and potential tuition increases into account. The AI ensures that savings contributions align with what truly matters to you.

Savings Beyond the Numbers

Predictive savings plans aren't just about crunching numbers—they're about helping you build a sustainable financial future. By offering insights into spending habits, these plans encourage smarter decisions. Generative AI can point out unnecessary expenditures, such as subscriptions you rarely use, and suggest reallocating those funds toward your goals.

For example, a couple using a predictive savings tool might discover they spend more on dining out than they realized. With this insight, they can choose to reduce those outings and allocate the savings toward their dream vacation. This proactive approach makes saving feel less like a sacrifice and more like a strategic choice.

The Role of Real-Time Data

Generative AI thrives on real-time data, making predictive savings plans incredibly responsive. These plans can track fluctuations in your income, expenses, and even external factors such as market conditions. When something changes, the AI updates your savings strategy instantly.

For example, if inflation rises and impacts the cost of everyday goods, your predictive savings plan can adjust your monthly contributions to ensure you're still progressing toward your goals.

Similarly, if you receive an unexpected bonus, the AI might recommend allocating a portion to boost your savings or pay off debt.

This constant evolution ensures that your savings plan remains current, aligning it with both your present circumstances and future aspirations.

Building an Emergency Fund

An essential component of any financial plan is an emergency fund, and predictive savings plans excel in this area. By analyzing your income stability and typical monthly expenses, Generative AI can estimate the amount you need for a reliable safety net. For instance, if you're in a high-income but volatile job, the AI might suggest a larger emergency fund to account for potential income gaps. On the other hand, someone with a stable salary and minimal expenses might require a smaller fund. These tailored recommendations help you feel prepared without overextending your budget.

The Psychological Benefits of Predictive Savings

Saving money is as much about mindset as it is about math. Generative AI helps alleviate common psychological barriers to saving, including procrastination and the fear of financial insecurity.

By breaking down savings goals into manageable, bite-sized contributions, predictive savings plans make the process feel achievable. For example, instead of asking you to save $10,000 in a year, the AI might suggest setting aside $27.40 daily—a number that feels less intimidating and easier to incorporate into your routine.

Additionally, the AI provides encouragement by displaying progress in real-time. Seeing how small actions add up over time can be highly motivating, reinforcing positive financial habits.

Generative AI's Impact on Financial Inclusivity

Predictive savings plans also promote financial inclusivity by making sophisticated financial tools accessible to everyone, not just those with significant wealth. Many traditional financial advisors cater to high-net-worth individuals, leaving others underserved. Generative AI bridges this gap, offering personalized advice at a fraction of the cost.

For example, a young college graduate with limited savings can utilize a predictive savings app powered by Generative AI to create a realistic plan for establishing an emergency fund, repaying student loans, and eventually investing. The technology democratizes access to financial expertise, empowering individuals from all backgrounds to take control of their finances.

Transforming Savings for Businesses

Generative AI is not only revolutionizing personal finance but also creating groundbreaking opportunities for businesses to optimize their financial strategies. For many companies, particularly small and medium-sized enterprises (SMEs), managing cash flow and ensuring consistent savings are critical for long-term stability. Predictive savings plans, powered by Generative AI, address these challenges by enabling businesses to plan proactively, adapt dynamically, and maintain financial resilience.

Challenges Businesses Face in Saving

Businesses often operate in environments of uncertainty. Economic fluctuations, seasonal sales cycles, and unexpected expenses can strain cash flow and savings. For SMEs, these issues are exacerbated by limited access to capital and resources. Even profitable companies can face difficulties if they lack effective cash flow management strategies.

Common challenges include:

- **Seasonality:** Retailers, tourism operators, and agricultural businesses often experience income fluctuations tied to seasonal variations or shifts in market demand.
- **Unexpected Expenses:** Emergencies such as equipment failure or sudden market shifts can disrupt financial plans.
- **Inconsistent Cash Flow:** Payment delays from clients or fluctuating revenue streams make it challenging to allocate

funds for savings consistently.

Generative AI addresses these issues by creating predictive savings plans tailored to the unique circumstances of each business, offering solutions that go beyond traditional budgeting tools.

Predictive Savings for Seasonal Businesses

Seasonal businesses experience pronounced cash flow fluctuations, with peak periods generating high revenue and off-seasons resulting in slower income. Generative AI helps these businesses prepare for leaner months by predicting cash flow patterns and automating savings during periods of high revenue.

For example:

- **Peak-Season Planning:** During profitable months, AI analyzes the business's revenue and suggests saving a specific portion of the earnings. This reserve is designated for covering operating costs during periods of low revenue.
- **Expense Management:** The AI identifies high-cost periods and recommends adjusting operational expenses to preserve more capital for savings.
- **Scenario Modeling:** AI-powered tools simulate various seasonal scenarios, such as demand surges or drops, allowing businesses to allocate resources optimally.

A small retail business selling winter sports gear, for instance, might experience a surge in sales during colder months. Generative

AI can recommend saving a portion of these profits to cover operational costs during the off-season, thereby reducing reliance on external financing, such as loans or credit lines.

Cash Flow Optimization

For businesses with inconsistent cash flow, predictive savings plans provide stability by smoothing out financial uncertainties. Generative AI evaluates the timing and amount of incoming and outgoing payments, creating a dynamic savings plan that aligns with the company's financial rhythms.

This might involve:

- **Automated Reserves:** The AI sets aside a portion of surplus cash during months with higher-than-average revenue.
- **Adjustable Contributions:** During months with lower income, savings contributions can be paused or minimized without derailing long-term financial goals.
- **Debt Management:** For businesses carrying debt, AI tools prioritize savings while ensuring timely loan repayments, helping maintain a healthy balance sheet.

An example of this is a digital marketing agency that invoices its clients every month. Generative AI could analyze payment patterns and suggest reserving funds from early-paying clients to cover late payments from others, ensuring steady cash flow for operations.

Forecasting and Emergency Preparedness

Unexpected events, such as economic downturns or industry disruptions, pose significant risks to businesses. Generative AI enhances financial preparedness by identifying potential risks and recommending strategies to mitigate them.

Key capabilities include:

- **Expense Forecasting:** The AI analyzes historical spending patterns and external trends to predict potential cost spikes.
- **Emergency Fund Allocation:** Businesses can use AI-driven insights to build dedicated reserves for emergencies, ensuring that unanticipated expenses don't derail operations.
- **Market Sensitivity Analysis:** Generative AI can simulate the impact of market changes, such as rising material costs or reduced consumer demand, helping businesses adjust their savings strategies accordingly.

For instance, a restaurant chain could utilize AI to forecast an increase in ingredient prices resulting from supply chain disruptions and allocate additional funds to offset these costs. This foresight enables businesses to navigate challenges without resorting to drastic measures, such as staff layoffs or service reductions.

Streamlining Long-Term Savings Goals

Generative AI is also instrumental in helping businesses achieve long-term financial objectives. Whether it's saving for expansion, upgrading technology, or building a new facility, predictive savings plans ensure steady progress toward these milestones.

Here's how:

- **Strategic Investment:** AI identifies periods of strong cash flow and suggests allocating a portion of savings into high-yield investment accounts or fixed-term deposits to grow reserves.
- **Capital Project Planning:** For significant expenses, such as new equipment or property, the AI creates a detailed savings timeline that accounts for inflation and potential financing options.
- **Risk Mitigation:** By analyzing historical data, Generative AI highlights potential obstacles to achieving savings goals, enabling businesses to address them proactively.

Consider a tech startup planning to launch a new product in two years. Generative AI might recommend gradually saving from revenue surpluses while forecasting the project's budgetary needs. This ensures that the company has sufficient funds when the launch date arrives, avoiding last-minute financial scrambling.

Strengthening Financial Discipline

One of the often-overlooked benefits of predictive savings plans is the financial discipline they instill. Generative AI automates savings, reducing the temptation to allocate funds to non-essential expenses. This consistency builds a financial cushion over time, enabling businesses to operate with greater confidence.

For example:

- AI can block certain discretionary expenses during periods of low revenue, directing those funds into a reserve account.
- Business owners can set specific savings targets, and the AI provides reminders or progress reports to keep them on track.

This disciplined approach fosters long-term stability, especially for businesses operating in unpredictable markets.

A Competitive Edge for Small Businesses

In a competitive market, businesses that effectively manage their finances often outlast those that don't. Generative AI gives small businesses a decisive advantage by:

- **Leveling the Playing Field:** Sophisticated financial tools that were once only accessible to large corporations are now available to smaller businesses through affordable AI-powered platforms.
- **Enhancing Decision-Making:** Real-time insights and predictive analytics enable smarter, faster financial decisions.
- **Reducing Dependency on External Financing:** By building robust savings plans, businesses reduce their reliance on loans or credit, lowering their own financial risk.

A local bakery, for example, might use predictive savings to gradually save for a second location, leveraging insights from Generative AI to identify the right time for expansion while maintaining financial stability.

The Future of Business Savings with Generative AI

As Generative AI technology continues to evolve, its applications in business savings will expand even further. We may see AI systems that not only predict financial needs but also negotiate better terms with suppliers, optimize tax strategies, or identify government grants and incentives that align with a company's savings goals.

For businesses of all sizes, predictive savings plans powered by Generative AI represent a shift toward more intelligent, more proactive financial management. By leveraging these tools, companies can build resilience, seize opportunities, and thrive even in challenging economic conditions. Whether it's stabilizing cash flow, preparing for emergencies, or achieving ambitious growth objectives, Generative AI is the key to transforming how businesses save.

THE FUTURE OF PREDICTIVE SAVINGS

Generative AI is just beginning to revolutionize the financial landscape, and its potential for transforming predictive savings plans continues to grow. As technology evolves, future advancements promise to make savings tools even more accurate, accessible, and impactful. These innovations will not only refine the way we save but also redefine what it means to be financially empowered.

Advancements in Forecasting Accuracy

One of the key areas of improvement lies in the precision of financial forecasting. As Generative AI models become more sophisticated, they will be capable of analyzing even larger datasets with greater accuracy. These datasets include macroeconomic trends, industry-specific financial patterns, and individual lifestyle data, creating an intricate web of insights.

Imagine an AI system that can anticipate financial challenges years in advance. For example, it might predict rising energy costs in your area and recommend increasing your savings to cover future expenses. Such foresight will allow users to prepare for financial distress in advance, thereby preventing it and ensuring greater stability.

Deeper Integration with Financial Ecosystems

Another promising development is the seamless integration of predictive savings tools with broader financial systems. Shortly, Generative AI could become a central hub connecting your bank accounts, credit cards, investment portfolios, and even payment systems.

For instance, a fully integrated system automatically detects when a bill is due and suggests allocating funds from your savings account to avoid late fees. It can also identify surplus cash flow in your checking account and transfer it to high-yield savings or investment accounts, optimizing every dollar in real-time.

This integration could also extend to financial institutions. Banks and fintech companies may collaborate to embed Generative AI-powered savings tools directly into their offerings, providing customers with a unified experience. By eliminating the need for separate apps or manual intervention, these systems will make saving effortless.

Enhanced User Experiences

Generative AI will also enhance the user experience, making predictive savings plans more intuitive and engaging. Future tools might feature voice-activated commands, gamified interfaces, and interactive dashboards that provide a clearer picture of your financial progress.

For example, imagine a savings app that speaks directly to you, offering real-time advice based on your spending habits. It might say, "You've spent less on dining out this month—consider directing those savings toward your vacation fund!" Such personalized interactions would foster a stronger sense of connection and motivation, encouraging users to stick to their financial goals.

In addition, gamification could make saving more rewarding. Users might earn badges or unlock incentives for reaching milestones, such as completing a six-month emergency fund. These features would turn saving into a positive and engaging activity rather than a chore.

Negotiating Better Financial Opportunities

Generative AI may also act as a financial advocate for users, identifying and securing better opportunities on their behalf. Imagine a savings app that doesn't just recommend where to save but actively negotiates higher interest rates or identifies exclusive investment opportunities based on your profile.

For example:

- **Negotiated Savings Rates:** The app could leverage its data insights to identify banks offering competitive rates and automatically transfer your funds to maximize returns.
- **Tailored Investment Opportunities:** Using predictive algorithms, the AI might suggest low-risk bonds for a conservative saver or high-growth stocks for a more adventurous investor. It could notify users about limited-time offers that align with their financial goals.

These features ensure that users are not only saving but also actively growing their wealth in the most efficient way possible.

Expanding Accessibility

As Generative AI continues to evolve, predictive savings tools will become more inclusive, catering to diverse financial situations and needs. Currently, many advanced financial tools are primarily targeted at tech-savvy or high-income individuals; however, future iterations will focus on bridging this gap.

For example, new tools could cater specifically to underserved communities by offering simplified interfaces, multilingual support, or tailored services for irregular streams, such as those used by freelancers and gig workers. By breaking down barriers to access, Generative AI will empower more people to take control of their finances and achieve their savings goals.

Anticipating Global Trends

Global economic trends will also shape the future of predictive savings. As sustainability and environmental concerns grow, Generative AI might integrate these factors into savings plans. For instance:

Predicting the cost of adopting green technologies, such as solar panels or electric vehicles.

Encouraging users to save for environmentally conscious investments, aligning financial goals with ethical values.

Additionally, in an increasingly interconnected world, AI could monitor geopolitical shifts, currency fluctuations, and trade policies to recommend savings adjustments for international travelers or businesses with global operations.

A VISION FOR FINANCIAL EMPOWERMENT

The future of predictive savings plans, driven by Generative AI, is one of unparalleled empowerment. With more intelligent forecasting, deeper integration, and enhanced user experiences, these tools will enable individuals and businesses alike to achieve their financial goals more easily. Beyond simply saving money, Generative AI will enable users to plan, adapt, and thrive in an ever-changing world.

By harnessing the full potential of Generative AI, we are moving toward a financial future where saving isn't just a routine task—it's a strategic and rewarding journey. Whether you're building an emergency fund, preparing for significant life events, or striving for long-term security, the next generation of predictive savings tools will be your most valuable ally.

AUTOMATING SAVINGS BASED ON BEHAVIOR AND GOALS

Saving money has always been an essential part of financial planning. However, sticking to a savings plan can be difficult, especially when life's unpredictable expenses and temptations to spend interfere. This is where Generative AI steps in, transforming the traditional savings process into a more innovative, more personalized, and automated experience. By understanding individual behaviors and goals, Generative AI can streamline the process of saving, ensuring consistent and efficient progress.

The Foundation of Automated Savings

At its core, automated savings is about creating systems that do the work for you. Generative AI takes this concept further by personalizing these systems. Unlike traditional savings tools that require manual input and rigid planning, AI learns about your habits, adapts to your financial situation, and automatically sets aside money in ways that align with your goals.

For example, instead of setting a fixed amount to save every month, AI can analyze your spending patterns and income fluctuations. If one month allows for more savings due to fewer expenses, the AI can automatically save more without requiring you to intervene. Conversely, during months with higher payments, it can scale back to ensure you don't feel financially strained.

How AI Understands Behavior

Generative AI is built to recognize patterns in data. By analyzing your financial habits, it learns how you typically spend, what your regular income looks like, and where there's potential for saving. For instance:

- Spending Categories: AI breaks down your expenses into categories like groceries, entertainment, utilities, and discretionary spending. This allows it to identify areas where you might be overspending and suggest reallocating funds to savings.
- Timing and Frequency: AI observes when you typically earn and spend money, helping it identify the best times to move funds into savings. If your income arrives bi-weekly, the AI can schedule savings transfers shortly after payday, when your account balance is highest.

- Psychological Barriers: Many people hesitate to save because they fear losing access to their money. AI addresses this by setting up small, incremental savings amounts that feel manageable and non-restrictive.

This ability to tailor its actions based on behavior makes Generative AI much more effective than traditional one-size-fits-all solutions.

Setting Goals with Generative AI

Automated savings becomes even more powerful when combined with clear financial goals. Generative AI helps you define and prioritize these goals, whether it's saving for a vacation, building an emergency fund, or planning for retirement. Once goals are established, the AI continuously monitors your progress and adjusts savings contributions to keep you on track.

For example, if you're saving for a vacation, AI can estimate the total cost, including travel, accommodation, and spending money. It then calculates how much you need to save each month to reach that amount by your desired timeline. If unexpected expenses delay your progress, the AI can recalculate and adjust the plan to ensure you still meet your goal.

Dynamic Adjustments

One of the standout features of AI-driven automation is its ability to adapt to changing conditions. Life is unpredictable, and financial plans often need to change. Generative AI ensures that your savings strategy remains flexible:

- **Adapting to Income Changes:** If your income increases due to a raise or bonus, AI can automatically allocate a portion of the extra funds to savings. Similarly, if income decreases, it can reduce contributions to ensure your essentials are covered.
- **Responding to Unexpected Expenses:** When emergencies arise, AI can temporarily pause or reduce savings contributions without derailing your overall plan. It prioritizes your immediate needs while maintaining long-term goals.

This dynamic approach eliminates the need for constant manual adjustments, making saving seamless and stress-free.

Removing the Need for Willpower

One of the biggest challenges in saving money is overcoming the temptation to spend. Generative AI takes willpower out of the equation by automating the process. Once your savings strategy is established, AI ensures that contributions are made regularly without requiring your involvement. This "set-it-and-forget-it" approach minimizes the risk of falling off track due to procrastination or impulsive decisions.

AI also helps to gamify the process, turning savings into a rewarding experience. For example, some platforms use AI to send encouraging updates about your progress, such as how close you are to reaching a goal or how much you've saved compared to last month. These small motivators can make a big difference in staying committed.

Integrating Automation into Everyday Life

Generative AI integrates seamlessly with your daily financial tools, such as banking apps and digital wallets. This integration makes it easy to automate savings without disrupting your routine. Some practical examples include:

- **Round-Up Features:** AI-powered apps round up every purchase to the nearest dollar and deposit the difference into your savings account. For instance, if you spend $4.75 on coffee, the app saves $0.25. These small contributions add up over time without being noticeable.
- **Smart Transfers:** AI schedules savings transfers based on your cash flow. If it detects a pattern where your account balance is consistently higher on certain days, it can automate transfers during those times to avoid overdrafts.
- **Goal-Specific Accounts:** AI can create and manage multiple savings accounts, each dedicated to a specific goal. For example, it might allocate funds to a vacation account, a car repair fund, and a general emergency fund simultaneously, based on your priorities.

Real-Life Applications of Automated Savings

The transformative impact of Generative AI on automated savings is best understood through real-world examples:

- **Helping Young Professionals Save:** A recent college graduate struggled to balance student loan payments and saving for a first apartment. By using an AI-driven savings app, the graduate set a goal to save $5,000 within one year. The AI analyzed monthly expenses, suggestereducingon non-essential spending, and automated savings contributions. Within 10 months, the goal was achieved ahead of schedule.
- **Family Budget Optimization:** A family of four used Generative AI to create a system for saving toward a family vacation. The AI tracked the household's monthly expenses and identified opportunities to reduce costs on groceries and entertainment. By automating these small savings, the family reached their vacation goal without feeling deprived.
- **Emergency Fund Building:** A freelancer with unpredictable income used Generative AI to build an emergency fund. The AI adjusted savings contributions based on the freelancer's earnings, saving more during high-income months and pausing during slow periods. This flexible approach allowed the freelancer to create a safety net without financial strain.

The Long-Term Impact of Automation

The benefits of automating savings go beyond immediate financial gains. Over time, this approach builds habits of consistency and discipline. It also reduces stress by eliminating the need for constant decision-making and ensures that progress is made even when life gets busy.

Moreover, Generative AI enhances transparency by providing detailed insights into how savings are accumulating. This level of visibility helps individuals feel more confident and in control of their finances, reinforcing positive behaviors.

Empowering Financial Freedom

Automated savings driven by Generative AI present a major step forward in personal finance. By understanding individual behaviors and aligning actions with goals, AI removes many of the traditional barriers to saving. Whether it's building an emergency fund, achieving a dream, or preparing for the future, AI-powered automation empowers individuals to take charge of their financial destiny with ease and confidence.

By embracing this technology, you not only simplify your savings journey but also unlock opportunities for greater financial freedom. With Generative AI as your partner, achieving your goals becomes less of a challenge and more of a certainty.

CASE STUDIES ON IMPROVED SAVINGS OUTCOMES USING GENERATIVE AI

Generative AI has transformed the way individuals and businesses approach savings. Its ability to analyze data, predict trends, and automate processes has led to countless success stories. This section highlights real-world examples of how Generative AI has helped people and organizations improve their financial outcomes. These case studies are drawn from various scenarios, showcasing the versatility of this technology in addressing diverse savings challenges.

Empowering Freelancers: Sarah's Success Story

Sarah, a freelance graphic designer, faced the common challenge of inconsistent income. Like many freelancers, her earnings fluctuated from month to month, making it difficult to stick to a savings plan. She often felt overwhelmed trying to decide how much to save, especially during months when her income was lower than expected. Sarah decided to use a Generative AI-powered financial planning app to address her challenges.

The app started by analyzing Sarah's past income and expenses. It identified her high-earning months and her spending patterns. Based on this data, the AI created a dynamic savings plan tailored to her unpredictable income. During months when her income was higher, the app recommended saving a larger portion, while during lean months, it reduced the amount she needed to set aside, ensuring she wasn't financially strained.

The AI also introduced an automated savings feature. It transferred funds to her savings account immediately after she received payments from clients. Sarah no longer had to make manual decisions, reducing the risk of forgetting or overspending. Over time, the AI adapted to changes in her income and suggested adjustments to her plan, helping her save more effectively without feeling restricted.

After two years of using the app, Sarah successfully built a robust emergency fund and saved enough to purchase a new laptop for her business. The confidence she gained from her improved financial situation also inspired her to take on larger projects and grow her career.

Building an Education Fund: The Johnson Family

The Johnsons, a middle-income family of four, wanted to save for their eldest daughter's college education. However, they struggled to balance their daily expenses with long-term savings goals. They turned to a Generative AI platform that specialized in family financial planning.

The AI began by analyzing their household finances, including their income, regular expenses, and discretionary spending. It projected the future cost of college tuition based on inflation rates and the timeline they provided. The platform then suggested a savings goal and a monthly contribution amount that fit their budget.

One unique feature of the AI was its ability to dynamically adjust savings contribution. For example, during months when the family received tax refunds or bonuses, the AI recommended increasing their savings for that period. During tougher months, it reduced the contributions without derailing their overall goal.

The platform also introduced the Johnsons to the concept of "micro-saving." It rounded up their everyday transactions, such as grocery purchases and gas payments, and transferred the spare change to their college fund. Though these amounts seemed small, they added up significantly over time.

By the time their daughter was ready for college, the Johnsons had exceeded their initial savings target. This success allowed them to cover her first year of tuition without taking on student loans. The AI's personalized guidance gave them the peace of mind that they were on track, even during financial ups and downs.

A Small Business Thrives: Sam's Retail Shop

Sam, the owner of a small retail shop, faced challenges common to many entrepreneurs. His business had seasonal peaks and valleys, with profits fluctuating significantly throughout the year. While he earned well during the holiday season, the slower months often left him struggling to manage expenses. Sam wanted to create a savings buffer for lean periods but didn't know where to start.

Generative AI provided the solution. Using a business-focused AI tool, Sam gained insights into his cash flow patterns. The tool analyzed sales data from previous years and identified seasonal trends. It then recommended setting aside a specific percentage of his peak-season profits into a savings account.

The AI also helped Sam track and reduce unnecessary expenses. It identified cost-saving opportunities in areas such as inventory management and utility usage. By reallocating these savings, Sam was able to build his financial buffer more quickly.

Another advantage of the AI was its ability to simulate different scenarios. For example, it showed Sam how his savings would grow under various conditions, such as increasing his contributions by just 2% during high-profit months. Seeing the potential outcomes motivated him to stick to the plan.

Within 18 months, Sam had enough savings to cover three months of operating expenses. This financial cushion allowed him to navigate an unexpected economic downturn without resorting to loans. The AI not only improved his financial resilience but also gave him the confidence to expand his business.

A Family's Journey to Debt-Free Living

The Andersons, a family with two working parents and three children, were burdened with credit card debt and struggling to save for the future. They felt trapped in a cycle of minimum payments and increasing interest rates. Generative AI offered them a way out.

The utilizeded an AI-powered debt management app that thoroughly analyzed their financial situation. The app prioritized paying off high-interest debts first while ensuring that they could still contribute to a small savings fund. It suggested a monthly repayment plan that aligned with their income and essential expenses.

The AI also provided personalized tips to reduce spending. For example, it identified that their grocery expenses were higher than average for a family of their size. It suggested meal-planning strategies and offered discounts on local grocery stores based on their shopping habits.

One unique feature of the app was its motivational feedback. It regularly updated the Andersons on their progress, showing how much interest they had saved and how close they were to being debt-free. This positive reinforcement kept them committed to the plan.

After three years of following the AI's guidance, the Andersons paid off all their credit card debt. They also managed to build an emergency fund, giving them financial stability they hadn't experienced in years. The AI's step-by-step approach made a daunting process feel manageable and achievable.

Automated Savings for Young Professionals

Emma, a recent college graduate, was new to managing her finances. She had a stable job bu struggled lt to save consistently due to he excessive social spending habits. She decided to try a Generative AI app recommended by a friend.

The app started by analyzing Emma's income and expenses. It set a realistic savings goal for her first year, focusing on building a small emergency fund. To make saving easier, the AI automated her savings by transferring a fixed percentage of her paycheck to a separate account before she could spend it.

What made the app unique was its ability to learn and adapt to Emma's lifestyle. For instance, it noticed that she spent more on dining out during weekends. Instead of imposing strict restrictions, it suggested small, manageable changes, like skipping one restaurant visit per month. These adjustments allowed Emma to save without feeling deprived.

The AI also introduced Emma to investment opportunities. Once her emergency fund reached a certain threshold, the app recommended low-risk investments to grow her savings. By the end of her first year, Emma had not only saved more than she thought possible but also taken her first steps into investing.

The Bigger Picture: Generative AI's Role in Savings

These case studies highlight the transformative impact of Generative AI on financial savings. From individuals to families and small businesses, the technology has proven its ability to address diverse challenges with personalized solutions. By leveraging predictive capabilities, dynamic planning, and automation, Generative AI has made saving more accessible, efficient, and effective.

The key takeaway from these examples is the importance of starting small and trusting the process. Generative AI provides the tools and insights needed to make informed decisions, adapt to changes, and stay on track toward financial goals. Whether it's a freelancer stabilizing their income, a family saving for education, or a business building resilience, the possibilities with Generative AI are endless.

CHAPTER 5

RISK MANAGEMENT WITH GENERATIVE AI

In the ever-changing world of finance, managing risks effectively is one of the most important aspects of maintaining stability and security. Risks can come from various directions—unexpected market changes, fraudulent activities, or even personal financial habits that leave gaps in planning. Generative AI, with its advanced ability to analyze, predict, and create solutions, offers a powerful way to manage these risks more efficiently and accurately. This chapter explores how Generative AI is changing the way we identify financial risks, prevent fraud, and optimize insurance strategies.

UNDERSTANDING RISK MANAGEMENT WITH GENERATIVE AI

Risk management involves identifying potential threats to financial stability and taking steps tmitigatece their impact. Traditionally, this process has relied on historical data, manual reviews, and fixed formulas. While these methods have been useful, they often fail to keep up with the speed and complexity of modern financial systems. Generative AI changes the game by not just analyzing past data but also generating new scenarios and solutions tailored to specific financial situations.

For example, consider a financial planner trying to prepare for an unpredictable market. Generative AI can simulate how a portfolio might perform under various conditions, such as a sudden drop in stock prices or an increase in interest rates. This helps decision-makers see potential outcomes and plan accordingly, long before any actual event occurs. By providing this level of foresight, Generative AI enables not more proactive risk management e than reactive management.

Identifying Financial Risks

One of the most significant contributions of Generative AI in risk management is its ability to identify risks that may not be immediately obvious. Traditional methods often focus on well-known risks, but Generative AI can uncover subtle patterns that hint at emerging threats.

For instance, in the world of investing, risks often come from market volatility or unexpected economic changes. Generative AI can analyze vast amounts of market data in real-time, spotting trends that might indicate future instability. This level of analysis allows financial institutions and individual investors to make adjustments before problems arise.

In personal finance, Generative AI can analyze an individual's spending and saving habits to highlight potential risks. If someone is overspending in certain areas or not saving enough for future needs, the AI can suggest adjustment to help ensuring a more secure financial future. It's like having a financial advisor who's always one step ahead.

Fraud Detection and Prevention

Fraud is one of the biggest challenges in finance, costing individuals and organizations billions of dollars annually. The rise of online transactions and digital banking has made fraud more complex and harder to detect. Generative AI provides a robust solution to this problem by offering advanced tools for fraud detection and prevention.

Unlike traditional systems, which rely on static rules to identify fraud, Generative AI uses dynamic models that adapt to new types of fraudulent behavior. It doesn't just look for patterns that match past fraud—it learns and evolves as new threats emerge. For example, it can analyze transaction data to detect unusual activity, such as a sudden series of high-value purchases on a credit card. The AI flags these activities for review, often catching fraud before it can cause significant damage.

Generative AI also excels at creating synthetic data to train its models. Synthetic data mimics real-life scenarios, including potential fraud cases, without requiring the use of sensitive personal information. This approach ensures the AI system is well-prepared to handle a wide range of threats while maintaining privacy and security.

Another critical application of Generative AI in fraud prevention is its ability to analyze behavioral patterns. By studying how users typically interact with financial platforms, the AI can detect when something unusual occurs, such as a login from an unfamiliar location or device. These insights enable financial institutions to act quickly, protecting their clients and their assets.

Insurance Optimization

Insurance is a vital part of financial risk management, helping individuals and organizations protect themselves from unforeseen events. However, the process of selecting and managing insurance policies can be overwhelming and inefficient. Generative AI offers a way to streamline and optimize this process, making insurance more accessible and effective.

One of the most significant ways Generative AI improves insurance is through personalized policy recommendations. Traditional insurance policies often take a one-size-fits-all approach, but Generative AI analyzes individual needs and circumstances to recommend tailored options. For example, an AI system could analyze a driver's behavior, such as how often and how safely they drive, to suggest a car insurance policy that matches their specific risk profile. This ensures that people aren't overpaying for unnecessary coverage or underinsured for critical risks.

Another area where Generative AI shines is in claims processing. Filing an insurance claim can be a long and frustrating experience, but AI can speed up the process significantly. By analyzing claim details and comparing them with historical data, the AI can assess the validity of a claim almost instantly. This reduces delays and ensures that legitimate claims are approved quickly.

In addition to improving efficiency, Generative AI helps insurance companies to detect fraudulent claims more effectively. It can analyze patterns in claim data to identify inconsistencies or red flags that might indicate fraud. For instance, if multiple claims are filed for similar damages within a short period, the AI might flag these for further investigation.

Real-Life Applications and Success Stories

To fully understand the potential of Generative AI in risk management, it is helpful to examine at real-world examples. One global insurance company used Generative AI to optimize its pricing models. By analyzing customer data and generating scenarios, the AI system identified ways to adjust premiums that benefited both the company and its clients. As a result, the company saw a 15% increase in customer satisfaction and a significant reduction in claim processing times.

Another example comes from the banking sector, where Generative AI was used to prevent credit card fraud. By analyzing transaction patterns, the AI detected fraudulent activities in real time, saving the bank millions of dollars and protecting its customers from financial losses.

Ethical Considerations in AI-Driven Risk Management

While the benefits of Generative AI in risk management are

clear, it's essential to address the ethical challenges that come with its use. Data privacy is a significant concern, as AI systems rely on vast amounts of personal information to function effectively. Organizations must ensure that this data is handled securely and responsibly to protect individuals' privacy.

Another challenge is the potential for bias in AI algorithms. If the data used to train an AI system contains biases, the AI's decisions may also be biased. For example, an insurance AI might unintentionally favor certain demographics over others when recommending policies. To avoid this, it's crucial to use diverse and representative datasets when training AI models.

Transparency is essential in AI-driven risk management. Users and regulators need to understand how AI systems make decisions, especially when those decisions have significant financial or ethical implications. Ensuring transparency builds trust and accountability, making AI tools more widely accepted and effective.

The Future of Generative AI in Risk Management

As technological innovation accelerates, the capabilities of Generative AI in risk management are set to expand in ways that will redefine financial security and preparedness. The future promises advancements that will make these systems smarter, faster, and more adaptable to evolving risks, offering solutions that are not only innovative but also highly practical for real-world applications. One area of significant growth lies in predictive accuracy. Current

Generative AI models already demonstrate an impressive ability to analyze patterns and forecast risks. However, future developments will likely integrate even larger datasets, such as global economic trends, social dynamics, and climate variables, to provide an even deeper understanding of potential threats. For instance, imagine an AI system capable of predicting the impact of natural disasters on global markets and providing financial institutions with preemptive strategies to minimize losses.

Additionally, we can expect a rise in context-aware AI systems. Unlike current models, which rely heavily on predefined data inputs, future Generative AI will be able to interpret broader, real-time contexts. This will allow systems to adjust to sudden changes, such as political instability or unforeseen economic downturns, with unmatched speed and precision. For example, businesses using such systems will be able to reallocate resources or adjust investment portfolios the moment early warning signs of a recession emerge.

Another promising advancement is the integration of hybrid AI frameworks. These frameworks will combine Generative AI with other types of artificial intelligence, such as reinforcement learning and explainable AI (XAI). The combination will offer not only advanced predictions but also greater transparency, helping users understand how the AI arrived at its conclusions. This transparency will be particularly crucial in regulatory environments, where accountability in decision-making ty is a top priority.

Automation and Personalization will also become more refined. Future Generative AI systems will likely automate even the most complex risk management processes, from identifying potential cybersecurity threats to optimizing insurance portfolios in real time. Automation will save valuable time for individuals and businesses while reducing human error. At the same time, the ability of AI to generate highly personalized risk management strategies will improve significantly. Tailored solutions for individuals, businesses, and industries will ensure a more accurate fit for specific needs, increasing overall effectiveness.

The global nature of risk management will also drive the evolution of Generative AI. In a world where risks are increasingly interconnected, such as pandemics, climate change, or international trade, AI systems must adopt a global perspective. Future models will analyze and cross-reference data from multiple regions, creating risk profiles that account for interconnected vulnerabilities. For example, a business operating in multiple countries could receive AI-generated strategies that address risks unique to each location while considering their broader impact on the organization.

Another critical future capability is real-time collaboration between humans and AI. While AI systems are becoming more autonomous, the human element remains vital in decision-making, especially in high-stakes financial scenarios. Future advancements will focus on creating seamless interfaces where AI can provide real-time suggestions while allowing human experts to guide the decision-making process. This collaboration will enhance trust in AI systems and ensure that users can rely on the technology for strategic planning.

Lastly, the democratization of Generative AI in risk management will make these tools accessible to a wider range of users. Currently, the most advanced AI solutions are primarily available to large corporations with substantial resources. Future innovations will drive down costs, making sophisticated risk management tools available to small businesses and even individuals. Imagine a small business owner using a cost-effective AI tool to predict cash flow challenges or a family relying on AI to adjust their savings strategy based on market shifts.

However, these advancements will come with their own set of challenges. Ethical considerations, such as ensuring fairness and addressing algorithmic bias, will become even more critical as Generative AI takes on a larger role. Robust regulatory frameworks will be needed to keep pace with technological progress, ensuring that AI systems are used responsibly and transparently.

IDENTIFYING FINANCIAL RISKS THROUGH GENERATIVE AI

Risk management is one of the most critical aspects of financial planning. Whether for individuals or organizations, the ability to foresee, assess, and address potential risks can mean the difference between financial success and disaster. Generative AI is revolutionizing how risks are identified, offering tools that go far beyond the capabilities of traditional methods. This part of the chapter explores how Generative AI identifies financial risks with unparalleled accuracy and efficiency.

A New Perspective on Risk Management

Generative AI brings a unique approach to risk management by not only analyzing historical data but also generating predictions and scenarios that highlight potential vulnerabilities. Traditional risk assessment methods often focus on what has happened in the past, using patterns to predict future risks. While this approach is valuable, it falls short in capturing the complexities of dynamic, ever-changing financial landscapes. Generative AI, on the other hand, uses its ability to simulate possibilities and generate new data to predict risks that might not be evident in historical trends.

For instance, consider a scenario where market conditions shift rapidly due to unforeseen global events. A traditional risk model might fail to adapt quickly enough to protect investments or financial plans. Generative AI, with its advanced simulation capabilities, can forecast a range of outcomes based on various influencing factors, enabling individuals and businesses to take preemptive action.

Dynamic Insights into Market Volatility

Market volatility is one of the most prominent risks faced by investors. The unpredictable nature of markets, influenced by factors such as political developments, natural disasters, or economic policies, can lead to significant financial losses. Generative AI is equipped to address this challenge by identifying subtle signals in the market that may indicate upcoming volatility.

By analyzing vast datasets that include historical market behavior, real-time news feeds, and economic indicators, Generative AI creates models that simulate how markets might respond to different scenarios. For example, it can evaluate how an unexpected increase in interest rates might affect various industries and suggest portfolio adjustments to minimize exposure.

This ability to provide dynamic, real-time insights into market movements empowers investors to make well-informed decisions. It also offers businesses a clearer understanding of how external factors could impact their operations and profitability.

Assessing Organizational Risks

Organizations face a multitude of risks, ranging from operational inefficiencies to external threats like cyberattacks or regulatory changes. Generative AI enhances traditional risk assessment by offering a holistic view of these risks, identifying both internal vulnerabilities and external pressures.

For instance, in a manufacturing company, Generative AI

could analyze supply chain data to identify potential disruptions. By simulating scenarios such as a delay in raw material shipments or changes in supplier pricing, the AI model can suggest strategies to mitigate these risks, such as diversifying suppliers or adjusting production schedules.

Generative AI can also evaluate employee behavior, financial performance, and compliance with regulations, providing organizations with actionable insights to strengthen their overall risk posture. For companies operating in highly regulated industries, such as finance or healthcare, these insights are invaluable in avoiding penalties and maintaining operational integrity.

Personalized Risk Analysis for Individuals

Generative AI isn't just for large organizations; it also offers significant benefits to individual financial planning. Every person's financial situation is unique, with varying goals, income levels, and risk tolerance. Generative AI personalizes risk assessments by analyzing an individual's financial habits, spending patterns, and future aspirations.

For example, a young professional planning to buy a home may face risks related to fluctuating interest rates or unexpected expenses. Generative AI can analyze their income, savings, and credit history to identify potential financial gaps and recommend strategies to address them. Similarly, for retirees managing their savings, the AI can simulate scenarios where healthcare costs rise or market downturns occur, helping them adjust their plans accordingly.

This level of personalization ensures that individuals are better equipped to handle uncertainties and make decisions that align with their long-term financial goals.

Detecting Emerging Risks

One of the standout features of Generative AI is its ability to detect emerging risks that may not yet be widely recognized. These risks often arise from new technologies, changes in consumer behavior, or shifts in economic conditions. By analyzing data from diverse sources, including social media trends, news articles, and industry reports, Generative AI identifies patterns that signal potential threats.

For instance, in the context of cybersecurity, Generative AI can analyze the frequency and nature of recent data breaches to predict which industries or organizations might be targeted next. Similarly, in the financial sector, it might detect subtle shifts in consumer spending habits that could indicate broader economic changes.

By identifying these emerging risks early, Generative AI gives individuals and organizations a critical advantage in preparing for and responding to challenges before they escalate.

Reducing Human Bias in Risk Assessment

Traditional risk assessment often relies on human judgment, which can be influenced by biases or limited perspectives. Generative AI mitigates this issue by providing an objective, data-driven analysis. It evaluates risks based solely on patterns and probabilities, without being swayed by emotions or preconceived notions.

For example, a financial advisor may overlook certain investment opportunities due to a lack of familiarity or personal preference. Generative AI, however, considers a broader range of data and generates insights that might have been missed, ensuring that decisions are based on comprehensive and accurate information. This objectivity is particularly valuable in high-stakes environments where even small errors in judgment can have significant consequences.

Scalability and Efficiency

Another key advantage of using Generative AI for identifying financial risks is its scalability. Unlike traditional methods, which often require significant time and resources to analyze data, Generative AI processes vast amounts of information quickly and efficiently. This capability makes it an ideal solution for large organizations managing complex financial portfolios, as well as individuals seeking timely advice.

For instance, a global corporation can use Generative AI to monitor risks across multiple markets and subsidiaries simultaneously. Meanwhile, an individual investor can benefit from the same technology to receive tailored insights into their personal finances. This scalability ensures that the benefits of Generative AI are accessible to a wide range of users.

Practical Applications in Financial Planning

The practical applications of Generative AI in risk identification extend to various areas of financial planning. For businesses, it can highlight operational risks such as supply chain vulnerabilities or regulatory non-compliance. For investors, it can forecast the impact of market fluctuations on their portfolios.

Generative AI also plays a crucial role in disaster preparedness, helping organizations and individuals anticipate the financial implications of events like natural disasters, cyberattacks, or economic downturns. By generating simulations and actionable insights, it enables proactive measures that minimize financial damage and ensure resilience.

The Future of Risk Identification

Generative AI is poised to play an even more transformative role in financial risk identification as technology continues to evolve. The advancements we foresee in this area will not only enhance the precision of risk analysis but also deepen the integration of AI into everyday financial decision-making processes. These developments promise to create a future where financial risks can be predicted and managed with unparalleled efficiency.

Sophisticated Simulations for Risk Prediction

One of the most exciting prospects for Generative AI in risk identification is the development of more sophisticated simulation models. Current AI systems already simulate market scenarios, project financial outcomes, and suggest mitigation strategies, but future iterations will go a step further. With advanced algorithms and faster processing capabilities, Generative AI could simulate complex multi-layered risks, such as simultaneous market downturns across global economies, coupled with shifts in consumer behavior.

For example, financial institutions might use such models to prepare for systemic risks, like a global recession sparked by a natural disaster or geopolitical conflict. By simulating various "what if" scenarios, organizations and individuals can develop more resilient financial plans that account for interconnected risks.

Deeper Personalization in Risk Analysis

Generative AI will also advance the personalization of financial risk assessments. Today, it tailors recommendations based on income, spending habits, and individual goals, but the future promises even deeper customization. AI systems could integrate diverse data sources—such as social media activity, real-time spending trends, and even emotional health indicators—to provide highly nuanced risk profiles.

Consider a young entrepreneur launching a tech startup. Generative

AI could combine financial records, market data, and industry insights to predict potential cash flow issues or investment shortfalls. It might also incorporate behavioral patterns, such as the entrepreneur's tendency to take risks, to refine its suggestions further. This level of detail ensures that advice is not only accurate but also practical and actionable.

Seamless Integration with Emerging Technologies

The future of Generative AI in risk management lies in its ability to integrate seamlessly with emerging technologies. For instance, Generative AI could collaborate with the Internet of Things (IoT) to monitor physical risks in real-time. Imagine a scenario where smart home devices detect environmental changes, like increased humidity levels, that could lead to property damage. The AI system could immediately alert homeowners about potential risks, suggest preventive measures, and even recommend optimized insurance coverage.

Similarly, wearable health technology could work alongside Generative AI to assess health-related financial risks. Devices monitoring heart rates, activity levels, and other metrics could feed data into an AI system, enabling it to predict healthcare costs or recommend insurance adjustments. This fusion of technologies allows for proactive risk identification tailored to specific life circumstances.

Improved Accuracy Through Diverse Datasets

As Generative AI evolves, access to more diverse and comprehensive datasets will enhance its accuracy. Financial risks are influenced by numerous factors, including global trends, individual behaviors, and environmental conditions. By drawing from wider datasets, AI models will be better equipped to recognize subtle patterns and predict risks that might otherwise go unnoticed.

For instance, future Generative AI systems might analyze data from unconventional sources like climate reports, political developments, or cultural shifts to anticipate risks. A corporation considering expansion into a new region could use such AI tools to assess the financial implications of local regulatory changes or cultural preferences.

Proactive Risk Management with Real-Time Insights

Real-time data processing will also become a hallmark of Generative AI in risk management. As the speed and volume of data generation increase, AI systems will be capable of delivering instant insights into emerging risks. For example, during a stock market crash, Generative AI could immediately identify which investments are most vulnerable and recommend reallocation strategies, helping investors act before losses escalate.

Similarly, businesses might rely on real-time AI insights to adjust operations in response to supply chain disruptions, currency fluctuations, or sudden shifts in customer demand. This ability to react quickly will provide a significant competitive advantage in navigating financial uncertainties.

Enhancing Collaboration Across Sectors

The future of Generative AI in risk management also involves enhanced collaboration across sectors. Financial institutions, technology providers, and regulators will need to work together to establish standards and ensure ethical implementation. Collaborative platforms could allow organizations to share anonymized data, enabling AI models to learn from broader datasets and improve their predictive capabilities.

For example, a consortium of banks might use Generative AI to analyze global economic trends collectively, identifying risks that impact the entire sector. By pooling resources and insights, these institutions could implement industry-wide measures to mitigate systemic risks.

Addressing Ethical Challenges

As Generative AI becomes more powerful, addressing ethical concerns will be crucial. Future advancements must prioritize transparency in decision-making, ensuring that AI-driven risk assessments are explainable and accessible to all users. This includes developing tools that help individuals understand why certain risks were flagged and how recommendations align with their goals.

Additionally, safeguarding data privacy will remain a top priority. The use of sensitive personal and financial information in AI systems necessitates strict security measures. Future developments in Generative AI must include robust protocols to prevent data breaches and misuse.

A Cornerstone of Modern Risk Management

The continuous improvement of Generative AI will cement its role as a cornerstone of modern risk management. By providing deeper insights, enhancing personalization, and integrating with cutting-edge technologies, it will redefine how financial risks are identified and mitigated. This evolution will empower individuals and organizations to navigate uncertainties with greater confidence, ensuring stability and growth in an unpredictable world.

The future of Generative AI in risk identification is not just about technological advancements; it's about creating a world where financial decisions are smarter, safer, and more inclusive. As we embrace these innovations, we pave the way for a more resilient and forward-thinking approach to managing risks.

FRAUD DETECTION AND PREVENTION

Fraud detection and prevention are critical components of modern financial security, as fraudulent activities continue to become more sophisticated. Generative AI has emerged as a revolutionary tool in this domain, offering advanced capabilities to identify, predict, and combat fraudulent activities. By learning from patterns in data and generating insights that traditional systems might overlook, Generative AI enhances the ability of individuals and organizations to protect themselves from financial threats.

Understanding Fraud in Financial Systems

Fraud has become an ever-evolving challenge in today's digital financial landscape, with new schemes appearing at an alarming rate. These fraudulent activities span a wide range, including identity theft, credit card fraud, phishing, insider trading, and money laundering. Each type of fraud carries distinct complexities, making detection and prevention a sophisticated task. Traditional fraud detection methods often fall short because they rely heavily on fixed rules or static data analysis. These systems are reactive rather than proactive, struggling to keep up with increasingly creative and adaptive fraud tactics.

Generative AI fundamentally changes this dynamic by leveraging its ability to analyze large volumes of data in real-time and learn from evolving patterns. Unlike static systems, Generative AI adapts to new data continuously, allowing it to predict and mitigate fraud even as tactics evolve.

For instance, credit card fraud often begins with perpetrators making small unauthorized transactions—sometimes only a few dollars—to test the validity of stolen card details. These seemingly insignificant actions are often missed by traditional rule-based systems, which prioritize large, out-of-the-ordinary transactions. Generative AI, however, excels at identifying even the most subtle irregularities. It analyzes transaction behavior dynamically, considering factors like timing, location, and spending history. For example, if a customer who typically makes small grocery purchases suddenly makes a late-night international transaction, the system flags this as a potential risk.

Moreover, Generative AI not only detects anomalies but also contextualizes them. It can compare the flagged behavior against a broader database of similar cases to determine whether the activity aligns with known fraudulent patterns. This nuanced approach minimizes the chance of overlooking fraud and reduces false positives, where legitimate transactions are mistakenly flagged as suspicious.

Adapting to Evolving Fraud Tactics

Another key advantage of Generative AI is its ability to anticipate new forms of fraud. Fraudsters are continuously innovating, developing schemes that exploit gaps in conventional detection systems. Traditional methods struggle to address this because they rely on predefined rules that do not account for emerging trends. Generative AI, on the other hand, learns from historical data and generates hypothetical scenarios, helping financial institutions prepare for potential threats even before they occur.

For example, in phishing schemes, fraudsters often use similar patterns of email or website design to trick users into providing sensitive information. Generative AI can be trained on a dataset of past phishing attempts and generate new examples of potential schemes. By doing so, it equips detection systems to identify fraudulent activities that might not yet exist but follow a logical progression based on past data.

Additionally, Generative AI incorporates behavioral analysis into its detection processes. In identity theft, fraudsters may attempt to mimic the behavior of legitimate users. For instance, they might use stolen credentials to access an online banking account. Generative AI can analyze behavioral biometrics, such as typing speed or navigation patterns, to differentiate between legitimate users and potential fraudsters. This ability to assess human behavior adds a vital layer of security.

Real-Time Fraud Detection in Action

Generative AI's real-time capabilities are crucial in combating fraud as it happens. Instead of analyzing transactions retrospectively, which can result in financial losses already being incurred, Generative AI evaluates activity the moment it occurs. For example, when a suspicious login attempt is detected from an unfamiliar location or device, the system can immediately freeze the account and notify the user, preventing unauthorized access.

One notable example is its application in preventing ATM card fraud. If a card is used at two geographically distant ATMs within a short period, Generative AI can analyze this behavior and identify it as highly unlikely for a single individual. Such cases are flagged instantly, and banks can take immediate action to prevent further unauthorized transactions.

Advantages Over Traditional Systems

Generative AI's ability to evolve alongside fraud tactics gives it a significant edge over traditional systems. Rule-based systems operate within rigid boundaries; for instance, they might flag transactions above a certain dollar amount as suspicious. While this approach may catch some fraudulent activities, it often results in either missing smaller-scale fraud or overwhelming financial institutions with false positives.

Generative AI bypasses these limitations by understanding not just isolated incidents but also the broader context. For example, rather than flagging a single large transaction, it evaluates the transaction as part of the user's overall behavior. If the transaction aligns with an ongoing pattern of suspicious activity, such as multiple failed login attempts followed by a large fund transfer, it is flagged. Conversely, if the large transaction is consistent with past behavior, it is likely deemed legitimate.

Case Study: Combating Insider Fraud

Insider fraud, where employees misuse access to exploit organizational resources, is notoriously difficult to detect because it often involves authorized actions performed in an unauthorized manner. Generative AI offers an effective solution by monitoring employee activity and identifying patterns that deviate from expected behavior. For instance, if an employee in a financial firm frequently accesses high-value accounts during odd hours without justification, the AI can flag this as a potential risk.

In one notable case, a multinational corporation implemented Generative AI to monitor internal transactions. Within months, the system uncovered an employee funneling small amounts of money from multiple accounts to an external entity. Traditional detection methods had overlooked this activity because each transaction fell within the threshold of authorized limits. Generative AI, however, identified the abnormal frequency and pattern of these transactions, leading to an investigation and resolution of the fraud.

How Generative AI Works in Fraud Detection

Generative AI is powered by advanced algorithms, such as Generative Adversarial Networks (GANs) and Transformer models, which process large datasets and create predictive scenarios. These models excel at identifying anomalies that may indicate fraudulent activity. By training on historical data, Generative AI can understand what constitutes "normal" activity and then pinpoint deviations that suggest fraud.

For example, consider online banking transactions. A customer who usually conducts transactions within a certain geographical area suddenly logs in from a foreign location and transfers a large sum of money. Generative AI evaluates this activity against the customer's historical behavior and flags it as suspicious. This prompt identification allows banks to intervene quickly, minimizing potential losses.

Another innovative approach is the use of synthetic data. Generative AI creates simulated fraud scenarios to train detection systems, enabling them to recognize new forms of fraud even before they occur. This proactive strategy ensures that detection mechanisms stay ahead of evolving threats.

Real-Time Monitoring and Alerts

One of the most transformative aspects of Generative AI in fraud prevention is its ability to monitor transactions in real-time. Traditional systems often detect fraud only after the fact, which can lead to significant financial damage. Generative AI, however, evaluates transactions as they happen, providing instant alerts when suspicious activity is detected.

For instance, an e-commerce platform might use Generative AI to monitor transactions. If a pattern emerges where multiple high-value purchases are made using a single credit card in a short period, the system generates an alert. This early warning system enables businesses to act immediately, either by blocking the transaction or contacting the cardholder for verification.

Reducing False Positives

A common challenge in fraud detection is the issue of false positives, where legitimate transactions are flagged as fraudulent. This can frustrate customers and erode trust in financial institutions. Generative AI significantly reduces false positives by analyzing transaction patterns more accurately and understanding the nuances of individual customer behavior.

For example, a traditional rule-based system might flag any large transaction as potentially fraudulent. Generative AI, on the other hand, takes into account the customer's previous spending patterns, location, and account activity to make a more informed decision. If the transaction aligns with past behavior, such as booking a vacation during the holiday season, it is less likely to be flagged.

Applications Beyond Traditional Banking

Fraud detection with Generative AI extends beyond banking to other industries like insurance, retail, and cryptocurrency. In insurance, fraudulent claims are a persistent issue, often requiring extensive investigation. Generative AI streamlines this process by quickly analyzing claims data, identifying inconsistencies, and flagging suspicious cases. This not only reduces losses but also improves efficiency.

In the cryptocurrency world, where transactions are anonymous and decentralized, fraud detection poses unique challenges. Generative AI addresses these by analyzing blockchain activity to identify unusual transaction patterns, such as rapid transfers between multiple wallets or sudden spikes in trading volume. These insights help platforms combat money laundering and other fraudulent activities.

Case Study: Protecting Online Payments

To illustrate the effectiveness of Generative AI, consider an online payment gateway that integrates this technology. Before its implementation, the company experienced frequent chargebacks due to fraudulent transactions. By adopting Generative AI, the system began analyzing customer behavior in real-time, identifying subtle changes in purchasing habits that indicated stolen credit card usage. Within months, the gateway reported a 50% reduction in fraudulent transactions and a significant decrease in chargebacks, saving millions of dollars.

Enhancing Security Through Collaboration

Fraud detection and prevention also benefit from collaborative efforts among organizations. Generative AI facilitates this by enabling secure data sharing while maintaining privacy. Financial institutions can share anonymized data to improve fraud detection models, making them more robust against emerging threats. For example, banks in a specific region might share data on phishing scams, helping each other recognize and block fraudulent attempts more effectively.

Challenges and Ethical Considerations

While Generative AI provides powerful tools for fraud detection, it is not without challenges. One concern is the potential for bias in AI models, which may lead to unfair targeting of certain demographics. For instance, if training data disproportionately represents fraudulent activity in a particular region, the AI might unfairly flag transactions from that area as suspicious.

To address this, financial institutions must ensure that training data is diverse and representative. Regular audits of AI systems are also crucial to identify and correct biases.

Another challenge is the risk of adversarial attacks, where fraudsters attempt to manipulate AI systems. For example, they might deliberately conduct transactions in patterns designed to bypass detection. To counter this, Generative AI systems must continually adapt and improve their models to stay ahead of sophisticated attackers.

Building Customer Trust

Fraud detection systems must balance security with customer experience. Overly aggressive systems that frequently block legitimate transactions can alienate users. Generative AI helps strike this balance by providing accurate, reliable fraud detection while minimizing disruptions. Clear communication with customers about the purpose of fraud prevention measures further enhances trust.

For instance, a bank that explains why a transaction was flagged and provides easy steps for resolution is more likely to maintain customer loyalty than one that simply declines transactions without explanation.

The Future of Fraud Prevention with Generative AI

As fraud tactics continue to evolve, so too must the tools used to combat them. Generative AI is uniquely positioned to lead this charge, with its ability to anticipate threats, adapt to new patterns, and provide real-time solutions. In the future, we can expect Generative AI to integrate seamlessly with other technologies, such as blockchain, to create even more secure systems.

One promising development is the use of AI-driven multi-factor authentication, where Generative AI analyzes not just passwords but also behavioral biometrics, such as typing speed or navigation patterns, to verify user identities. This layered approach significantly enhances security while maintaining user convenience.

INSURANCE OPTIMIZATION USING GENERATIVE AI

Insurance is a critical part of managing finances, providing a safety net for unexpected events. However, the traditional way of handling insurance has often been complicated, with confusing pricing, slow claim approvals, and generic policies that don't always meet individual needs. Generative AI is changing this by making insurance smarter, faster, and more tailored to customers' lives.

This technology works by processing huge amounts of data to uncover patterns and insights that were previously hard to find. With these capabilities, Generative AI is helping insurance companies improve how they set prices, approve claims, and design policies. For customers, this means better protection, quicker support, and more accurate costs.

Personalized Policies That Fit Your Needs

One of the biggest issues with traditional insurance is the "one-size-fits-all" approach. Policies are often created for broad groups of people, ignoring individual needs. Generative AI fixes this by helping insurance companies understand their customers on a deeper level.

For example, instead of charging everyone in the same age

group the same price for life insurance, Generative AI can analyze factors like a person's lifestyle, hobbies, and health records. This allows insurers to offer policies that are more relevant and fairer. A person who exercises regularly and eats healthily might pay less for health insurance because their lifestyle lowers their risk.

Similarly, homeowners in areas prone to hurricanes can benefit from policies that consider the specifics of their location. Generative AI can look at weather data, building materials, and even nearby infrastructure to offer a policy tailored to their unique risks. This personalization gives customers peace of mind knowing they have the right kind of coverage.

Faster and Stress-Free Claims

Filing an insurance claim has traditionally been a frustrating process, often involving long delays and confusing paperwork. Generative AI makes this easier by speeding up the entire process.

When a claim is submitted, AI tools can instantly verify whether it aligns with the policy's terms. For example, if a homeowner files a claim for water damage, the AI can check weather data to confirm a storm occurred and analyze images of the damage to estimate repair costs. This ensures claims are processed quickly and accurately, reducing the time customers spend waiting.

Generative AI also helps during emergencies. After a major event like a flood or earthquake, insurance companies often face an overwhelming number of claims. AI systems can quickly analyze the scale of the damage and prioritize the most urgent cases, ensuring help reaches those who need it most.

Making Pricing Fairer

Pricing insurance policies has always been a challenge. Traditional methods often rely on historical data, which doesn't always reflect a person's current situation. Generative AI changes this by using real-time information to set prices that are fairer and more accurate.

For instance, auto insurers can use telematics devices to track a customer's driving habits, such as how often they brake hard or exceed the speed limit. Drivers with safer habits can receive discounts, encouraging good behavior while saving money. This approach benefits both the insurer, by reducing risk, and the customer, by lowering costs.

In health insurance, wearable devices like fitness trackers can provide valuable data on activity levels, heart rates, and sleep patterns. Generative AI uses this information to offer discounts to healthier individuals or recommend coverage that fits their needs. For example, someone training for a marathon might receive advice on a plan that includes sports injury coverage.

Detecting Fraud and Saving Costs

Fraud is a major issue in the insurance industry, costing billions each year. Generative AI helps solve this problem by spotting unusual patterns in claims that may suggest dishonest behavior.

For example, if someone submits multiple claims for similar damages across different insurers, the AI system can flag this as suspicious. It can also compare claims to industry benchmarks. If a claim for car repairs is significantly higher than average, it might signal an attempt to inflate costs. By catching fraud early, insurers save money and can offer better rates to honest customers.

Improving Communication and Support

Generative AI also improves how insurers interact with their customers. Many companies now use AI-powered chatbots to provide real-time support. These chatbots can answer questions, guide customers through filing claims, and even suggest policy updates based on recent life changes.

For example, if a customer gets married, a chatbot might recommend updating their life insurance policy to include their spouse. This proactive approach ensures customers always have the right coverage without needing to navigate the system alone.

Building a Better Future for Insurance

The changes Generative AI brings to the insurance industry aren't just about making things easier today—they're also about preparing for tomorrow. As AI continues to improve, insurers will be able to predict risks more accurately, respond faster to crises, and create policies that adapt as people's lives change.

For customers, this means insurance will feel less like a burden and more like a helpful service designed to protect what matters most. For insurers, Generative AI offers a way to build stronger relationships with their customers while staying competitive in a rapidly changing world.

Transforming Policy Pricing with Generative AI

Insurance pricing has long been a point of contention for customers. Traditional models rely on generalizations, leading to premiums that may not accurately reflect individual circumstances. Generative AI changes this by introducing dynamic pricing strategies that consider real-time data.

For instance, in auto insurance, Generative AI can analyze driving behaviors through connected devices, offering drivers with safer habits lower premiums. Similarly, in health insurance, wearable technology can provide insights into lifestyle choices, enabling insurers to adjust premiums based on healthy behaviors. This approach ensures that customers pay for what they actually need, rather than being grouped into broad categories.

Moreover, Generative AI can predict potential risks by analyzing historical claims and identifying trends. For example, it might determine that individuals living in areas prone to flooding should have specific types of coverage, guiding both the insurer and the policyholder toward better-informed decisions. This level of personalization builds trust and enhances customer satisfaction.

Streamlining the Claims Process

Filing an insurance claim can be a tedious and time-consuming process, often involving extensive paperwork and back-and-forth communication. Generative AI simplifies this by automating key stages of the claims process.

When a claim is submitted, Generative AI can quickly verify its validity by cross-referencing policy details and historical claims data. For example, in the case of a car accident, AI tools can assess photographic evidence of damage, analyze police reports, and compare these inputs to the terms of the insurance policy. This reduces the time required to process claims, often from weeks to just days.

In addition to speeding up claims processing, Generative AI minimizes the potential for fraud. By detecting inconsistencies in submitted data or identifying patterns that suggest fraudulent behavior, AI tools protect both insurers and policyholders from financial loss. For instance, if a claim is unusually high compared to similar incidents in the same area, the AI system can flag it for further review, ensuring fairness in payouts.

This technology also improves communication between insurers and customers. Chatbots powered by Generative AI can provide real-time updates on claim statuses, answer frequently asked questions, and guide users through the process of filing claims. This level of transparency fosters trust and reduces frustration for policyholders.

Personalized Insurance Solutions

One of the most significant contributions of Generative AI to the insurance industry is its ability to deliver personalized solutions. Insurance is not a one-size-fits-all product, and Generative AI ensures that every policy is tailored to the unique needs of the individual or business.

For instance, small businesses often struggle to find insurance that adequately covers their specific risks without being overly expensive. Generative AI analyzes the industry, location, and operational data of a business to craft a policy that provides optimal coverage at a reasonable cost. This personalized approach is particularly beneficial for niche industries or startups, where traditional policies may not address specific needs.

For individuals, Generative AI can create policies that evolve over time. For example, a young family might initially focus on health and life insurance. As their circumstances change, such as buying a home or starting a business, the AI can adjust their policies to include property insurance or liability coverage. This adaptability ensures that coverage keeps pace with life's transitions, offering comprehensive protection without unnecessary costs.

Enhancing Customer Experiences

Generative AI is not only revolutionizing operational efficiency but also elevating customer experiences in the insurance industry. Today's consumers expect speed, accuracy, and personalization, and Generative AI delivers on all fronts.

Through predictive analytics, Generative AI anticipates customer needs and proactively suggests solutions. For instance, if a homeowner's insurance policy is about to lapse, the AI system can send a reminder and provide renewal options tailored to any changes in the homeowner's circumstances. Similarly, during natural disasters, AI-powered tools can quickly identify affected customers and expedite claims processing, providing much-needed support during critical times.

Generative AI also enables insurers to engage customers more effectively through multiple communication channels. Whether it's a chatbot answering questions on a website, a personalized email with policy recommendations, or a mobile app that tracks claims, AI ensures that every interaction is seamless and efficient. This level of service not only enhances satisfaction but also fosters loyalty in a competitive market.

Risk Assessment and Fraud Prevention

Insurance relies heavily on accurate risk assessment, and Generative AI excels in this area. By analyzing vast amounts of data, it identifies subtle patterns and trends that traditional methods might overlook. For instance, in life insurance, Generative AI can analyze medical records, genetic data (where permissible), and lifestyle factors to provide a more accurate assessment of risk.

This detailed analysis extends to fraud prevention. Fraudulent claims cost the insurance industry billions of dollars annually, impacting both providers and honest customers. Generative AI addresses this challenge by generating models that detect anomalies and predict fraudulent behavior.

For example, in property insurance, an AI system might notice a spike in claims for roof damage in a specific area following a minor storm. By cross-referencing meteorological data and photographic evidence, the system can determine whether these claims are legitimate. This proactive approach not only saves money but also deters fraudulent activities.

Building Resilience in the Industry

The insurance industry is inherently reactive, responding to events after they occur. Generative AI shifts this paradigm by enabling insurers to take a more proactive approach. For example, by predicting weather patterns and potential natural disasters, insurers can advise policyholders on preventive measures, reducing the likelihood of claims and fostering a safer environment.

This resilience extends to business operations as well. Generative AI helps insurers optimize their resources, from staffing to financial reserves, ensuring they are prepared for large-scale events. For instance, during a hurricane, AI systems can predict areas most likely to be affected and allocate adjusters and funds accordingly. This level of preparation minimizes disruption and enhances the industry's ability to respond effectively.

Ethical Considerations in Insurance Optimization

While the benefits of Generative AI are undeniable, it's important to address ethical considerations, particularly in the context of insurance. The use of personal data, such as medical records or driving habits, raises concerns about privacy and consent. Insurers must ensure that data is collected and used transparently, with explicit consent from policyholders.

Another ethical challenge is avoiding bias in AI models. For example, if an AI system disproportionately assigns higher premiums to certain demographics, it could reinforce systemic inequalities. To mitigate this risk, insurers must continuously monitor and refine their AI systems, ensuring fairness and accountability.

The integration of Generative AI into insurance optimization is still in its early stages, but its potential is immense. As technology continues to evolve, we can expect even greater levels of personalization, efficiency, and customer engagement. From enabling real-time claims processing to crafting dynamic policies that adapt to changing needs, Generative AI is set to redefine the insurance industry.

For customers, this transformation promises better value, more transparency, and faster service. For insurers, it offers a competitive edge in an increasingly digital world. As both parties embrace this technology, the future of insurance will undoubtedly be smarter, fairer, and more efficient.

CHAPTER 6

TAX OPTIMIZATION

REVOLUTIONIZING TAX PLANNING WITH GENERATIVE AI

Tax optimization has always been a challenging yet essential aspect of managing finances. For both individuals and businesses, taxes represent a significant financial obligation, often requiring meticulous planning to minimize liabilities without breaching compliance. The complexity of tax codes, paired with their constant evolution, makes effective tax management daunting for even the most experienced professionals.

Generative AI offers a transformative approach to this long-standing challenge. By leveraging its ability to process vast amounts of financial data and detect intricate patterns, it reshapes how taxes are handled. Traditional tax solutions are often rigid, applying standard formulas and rules to predictable scenarios. In contrast, Generative AI operates with a level of flexibility and intelligence that allows it to adjust to the unique needs of every user.

For businesses, Generative AI goes beyond simple calculations to create comprehensive tax strategies. It evaluates spending habits, revenue streams, and industry-specific deductions, crafting a plan that aligns perfectly with operational goals. Meanwhile, for individuals, it analyzes personal financial behaviors, highlights potential savings opportunities, and ensures that deductions and credits are fully maximized.

What sets Generative AI apart is its ability to adapt as circumstances change dynamically. Life events such as a career shift, a new investment, or the birth of a child can alter a person's tax liabilities significantly. Generative AI takes these changes into account in real time, continuously recalculating and providing updated recommendations to ensure financial plans remain efficient and compliant.

By simplifying the complexities of tax codes and offering precision-driven advice, Generative AI is not just making tax planning easier—it is revolutionizing it. With this technology, users can achieve better control over their financial responsibilities while ensuring compliance with ever-changing regulations.

How Generative AI Simplifies Tax Management

Generative AI's strength lies in its ability to analyze vast amounts of data, identify patterns, and create customized solutions. This capability is particularly impactful in tax planning, where small details can lead to significant savings.

First, Generative AI helps interpret complex tax codes. Tax laws are often intricate, filled with technical jargon and region-specific nuances that can confuse even seasoned accountants. AI systems trained on these codes can distill the information into simple, actionable recommendations, making tax planning accessible to anyone.

For example, an AI system might analyze your spending patterns and suggest deductions you may not have considered, such as energy-efficient home upgrades or educational expenses.

By providing clear explanations of these opportunities, the system empowers users to make informed decisions without needing to understand every detail of the law.

Moreover, Generative AI is not static. It continuously learns from user behavior and adapts its recommendations to evolving financial conditions. For instance, if your income fluctuates, the system can automatically adjust its strategies, ensuring you're always in the best possible position.

Personalized Tax Strategies for Every Situation

One of the most valuable aspects of Generative AI is its ability to personalize tax strategies. Whether you're a freelancer, a small business owner, or a retiree, AI can tailor its advice to your unique financial situation.

For individuals, this might mean identifying deductions related to home office expenses, charitable donations, or medical costs. For businesses, the focus could shift to optimizing depreciation schedules, utilizing industry-specific credits, or restructuring operations to reduce taxable income.

Take, for instance, a small business owner who struggles to keep track of deductible expenses. Generative AI can automatically categorize transactions, flagging those that qualify as deductions. By the end of the year, this business owner has a clear list of deductible items, saving time and ensuring no opportunity is missed.

In more complex scenarios, such as international business operations, Generative AI can analyze cross-border tax regulations to minimize liabilities. It identifies tax treaties, calculates potential savings, and ensures compliance with local laws in multiple jurisdictions.

Real-Time Tax Planning: Staying Ahead of the Curve

A key challenge in tax optimization is keeping up with changes in tax laws. Governments frequently update regulations, introduce new deductions, or alter existing ones. Missing these updates can result in lost opportunities or even compliance issues. Generative AI solves this problem by providing real-time tax advice.

For instance, if a government introduces a tax credit for electric vehicles, a Generative AI system could immediately alert users who qualify. It might also calculate the potential savings and suggest how to adjust financial plans to take full advantage of the credit. This level of proactive advice ensures users are always ahead of the curve.

Beyond identifying opportunities, real-time insights also protect against risks. Generative AI can scan for errors in tax filings or flag unusual transactions that might draw the attention of tax authorities. By addressing these issues before submission, users can avoid penalties and audits.

The Role of Generative AI in Compliance

Compliance is a cornerstone of tax management. Errors in filings or failure to follow regulations can lead to fines, legal complications, and reputational damage. Generative AI plays a critical role in ensuring accuracy and compliance by cross-referencing financial activities with applicable laws. One way AI achieves this is through automated data analysis. By reviewing every transaction in a financial portfolio, the system ensures that all entries align with tax codes. For example, it might identify a business expense incorrectly categorized as personal, correcting the error before it becomes an issue.

Additionally, Generative AI generates detailed reports that provide transparency into the tax planning process. These reports not only simplify audits but also help users understand the rationale behind each recommendation, fostering trust in the system.

Success Stories: How Generative AI Transformed Tax Strategies

Real-world examples highlight the transformative potential of Generative AI in tax optimization. These stories illustrate how individuals and businesses have used AI to improve accuracy, save money, and streamline their tax processes.

One example involves a single parent with multiple income streams, including a side hustle and rental property. Managing taxes across these sources was a constant struggle. After adopting a Generative AI-based tool, the parent received detailed advice on deductible expenses, optimal tax brackets, and ways to minimize liabilities. The result was a simpler filing process and thousands of dollars in annual savings.

In another case, a medium-sized enterprise faced challenges in navigating complex tax regulations across several states. The company's finance team implemented Generative AI to analyze regional tax laws and identify applicable credits. By restructuring certain operations based on AI recommendations, the company reduced its tax burden by 15% while maintaining compliance.

Beyond Savings: Building Long-Term Tax Strategies

Generative AI isn't just about reducing taxes in the short term; it also helps users develop sustainable, long-term strategies. By analyzing historical data and projecting future trends, the system creates comprehensive plans that align with both current goals and anticipated changes.

For example, a young professional planning for retirement might use Generative AI to explore the tax advantages of contributing to a Roth IRA versus a traditional IRA. The system could project potential savings over decades, helping the individual choose the option that maximizes long-term benefits.

Similarly, for businesses planning major investments, Generative AI can evaluate the tax implications of different financing options. Whether it's leasing versus purchasing equipment or expanding into new markets, AI ensures that every decision is made with tax efficiency in mind.

Ethical Considerations in AI-Driven Tax Optimization

While the benefits of Generative AI are immense, it's important to address the ethical considerations that come with its use. One key issue is data privacy. Tax optimization requires access to sensitive financial information, making it crucial to use AI systems that prioritize security and comply with data protection laws.

Bias is another concern. If an AI system is trained on incomplete or unrepresentative data, it might produce recommendations that favor certain groups over others. Developers must continuously refine these systems to ensure fairness and inclusivity. Finally, there's the question of over-reliance. While Generative AI provides invaluable insights, users should retain a basic understanding of their tax responsibilities. AI should complement human judgment, not replace it entirely.

The Future of Tax Optimization with Generative AI

Generative AI is poised to redefine the future of tax management in ways that extend far beyond its current capabilities. As this technology advances, it will unlock more precise and sophisticated approaches to tax optimization, making the process not only more effective but also seamlessly integrated into daily financial operations.

One significant area of growth lies in hyper-personalized recommendations. Future Generative AI systems will analyze not just financial transactions but also broader contextual data, such as career trajectories, lifestyle choices, and long-term financial goals. By combining these insights, AI could craft highly tailored tax strategies that adapt effortlessly to each user's evolving circumstances.

Integration with financial institutions is another transformative frontier. Generative AI could become the backbone of a connected financial ecosystem, where banks, investment platforms, and tax software work in harmony. This interconnectedness would allow AI to access real-time data across various platforms, streamlining the tax process and ensuring decisions are informed by the most up-to-date information.

Moreover, as governments increasingly adopt digital infrastructure, collaboration between Generative AI systems and tax authorities could lead to a more streamlined and transparent tax environment. AI could pre-fill tax forms using verified financial data, reduce errors, and even resolve compliance issues before filings are submitted. This proactive approach would save time for taxpayers while reducing administrative burdens for tax agencies.

Blockchain technology also holds immense promise when paired with Generative AI. By securely storing tax-related records on decentralized ledgers, blockchain ensures data integrity and simplifies audits. This level of transparency would make disputes over tax filings less common, as both taxpayers and authorities would have access to an immutable record of transactions.

Looking further ahead, AI-powered virtual assistants could fully automate the tax process. These systems could handle everything from analyzing financial data to filing returns, delivering a hands-off experience for users. With natural language processing capabilities, these virtual assistants could interact with users in an intuitive way, answering questions, providing real-time updates, and even offering tax-saving suggestions.

The future of tax optimization with Generative AI is not just about making the process easier—it's about transforming it into a proactive, intelligent, and fully integrated aspect of financial life. By harnessing these advancements, individuals and businesses alike will be better equipped to navigate the complexities of tax management with confidence and efficiency.

AI IN TAX PLANNING AND DEDUCTION MAXIMIZATION

Tax planning has always been a critical aspect of managing finances, yet it is often seen as complex and overwhelming. With the arrival of Generative AI, this essential task is being reimagined, offering unprecedented precision and simplicity. Generative AI is a transformative technology that can analyze vast amounts of financial data, identify tax-saving opportunities, and simplify compliance with tax regulations, all while tailoring strategies to individual needs. We will explore how Generative AI reshapes tax planning, helping individuals and businesses maximize deductions and streamline their tax processes.

Transforming Tax Planning with Generative AI

Tax planning typically involves a deep understanding of tax codes, financial behaviors, and strategic foresight. Generative AI simplifies this by acting as a digital assistant, capable of learning, adapting, and providing personalized recommendations. Unlike traditional methods, which rely on human expertise to comb through complex rules and numbers, Generative AI leverages advanced algorithms to spot opportunities and ensure compliance.

At its core, Generative AI identifies patterns within your financial activities. It considers your income, expenses, investments, and lifestyle choices to craft a tax strategy tailored specifically for you. By learning from historical data and predicting future trends, it can optimize your tax liability while ensuring that you meet regulatory requirements.

Personalized Tax Strategies

Generative AI shines in its ability to create highly customized tax plans. Every individual or business has unique financial circumstances, and a one-size-fits-all approach rarely works.

AI takes into account personal details such as income levels, spending habits, and investment portfolios to design strategies that align with specific goals.

For example, a small business owner might benefit from deductions related to office equipment or travel expenses. Generative AI identifies these opportunities by analyzing detailed financial records and matching them to relevant tax provisions. Similarly, for an individual taxpayer, the AI might suggest ways to utilize retirement savings contributions or charitable donations to reduce taxable income.

The personalization doesn't stop at deductions. Generative AI can also recommend optimal filing statuses, estimate quarterly tax payments for self-employed individuals, and provide insights into long-term tax planning.

Identifying Hidden Opportunities

Tax codes are often full of hidden opportunities for deductions and credits that many people overlook. These opportunities may vary depending on your industry, location, or personal circumstances. Generative AI excels at uncovering these hidden gems.

Consider a freelancer who works from home. While they may know about the home office deduction, they might not realize they can also deduct expenses related to internet services, professional software, or even a portion of their utility bills. Generative AI can scan through expenses and identify all eligible deductions, ensuring nothing is missed.

For businesses, AI can pinpoint industry-specific tax credits. A company that invests in renewable energy may qualify for energy efficiency tax credits, while a tech startup conducting research and development could benefit from R&D tax credits. Generative AI automates the process of matching expenses to these opportunities, making it easier for businesses to take full advantage of the tax code.

Automation for Efficiency

One of the greatest advantages of Generative AI is its ability to automate time-consuming aspects of tax planning. Tasks such as tracking expenses, categorizing transactions, and calculating deductions are handled seamlessly by AI-powered tools. This not only saves time but also minimizes the risk of human error.

Imagine a small business owner juggling multiple responsibilities. Generative AI can automatically track business expenses, categorize them into tax-deductible and non-deductible items, and provide a comprehensive report when it's time to file taxes. This eliminates the need for manual bookkeeping and ensures that no deductible expense is overlooked.

Automation also extends to tax form preparation. Generative AI can fill out forms based on the data it has analyzed, ensuring accuracy and compliance. This reduces the burden on taxpayers and allows them to focus on other important financial matters.

Scenario Analysis and Decision Support

Tax planning often involves making decisions with long-term consequences. Should you invest in a retirement account now or pay off debt? Would purchasing a property provide better tax benefits than renting? Generative AI can simulate different scenarios and provide insights to help you make informed decisions.

By analyzing historical data and projecting future trends, AI tools can show you the potential outcomes of various financial decisions. For instance, it might demonstrate how contributing to a Roth IRA today could lead to significant tax savings over the next decade. Alternatively, calculate the benefits of deferring income to the following tax year to reduce your current liability.

These simulations are invaluable for individuals and businesses seeking to optimize their financial strategies while minimizing tax burdens.

Staying Updated with Tax Regulations

Tax laws are constantly evolving, with changes that can impact deductions, credits, and compliance requirements. Keeping up with these changes is a challenge for most taxpayers. Generative AI addresses this by staying updated in real time, ensuring that your tax strategies remain relevant and effective.

For example, if a new tax law introduces incentives for electric vehicle purchases, AI can immediately identify whether you qualify and calculate the potential savings. Similarly, if regulations affecting small businesses change, the AI can adapt your tax plan to ensure compliance while maximizing benefits.

This adaptability is particularly useful for businesses operating in multiple jurisdictions, where tax rules may vary widely. Generative AI simplifies the process by consolidating and analyzing regulations from different regions, helping businesses navigate complex tax landscapes with ease.

Enhancing Accuracy and Reducing Risks

Accuracy is critical in tax planning. Errors can lead to penalties, audits, and even legal issues. Generative AI significantly reduces the risk of errors by automating calculations and cross-referencing data with tax codes.

For instance, AI can identify discrepancies in reported income, flagging potential issues before they escalate. It also ensures that deductions and credits are applied correctly, providing peace of mind to taxpayers. By acting as a virtual safety net, Generative AI enhances the accuracy and reliability of tax filings.

Real-Life Applications of Generative AI in Tax Planning

To understand the practical impact of Generative AI, let's consider some real-world scenarios:

- **Small Business Optimization:** A small retail business used

Generative AI to manage its tax planning. The AI tool analyzed sales data, identified eligible deductions for inventory and equipment, and prepared a detailed tax report. As a result, the business saved thousands of dollars in taxes and avoided penalties.

- **Individual Taxpayer Success:** A freelance graphic designer utilized Generative AI to streamline their tax process. The tool tracked expenses, categorized deductions, and suggested contributions to a retirement account. The AI's insights not only reduced their tax liability but also helped them plan for future financial goals.
- **Corporate Efficiency:** A multinational corporation implemented Generative AI to handle its complex tax obligations across multiple countries. The AI system consolidated data from various subsidiaries, identified regional tax credits, and ensured compliance with local regulations. This streamlined approach resulted in significant cost savings and improved audit readiness.

Ethical and Practical Considerations in Generative AI for Tax Planning

Generative AI holds great promise in simplifying tax planning, yet its implementation raises important ethical and practical questions that must be addressed to ensure safe and effective usage.

1. Data Privacy and Security

Generative AI systems rely on vast amounts of sensitive financial data to deliver tailored tax strategies. This data includes income records, expense patterns, and even investment details, making privacy a key concern. If improperly managed, this information could be exposed to unauthorized access, leading to significant financial and reputational harm for individuals and businesses.

To safeguard against such risks, it is critical to use AI tools that prioritize robust data protection measures. Encryption, anonymization, and access control are essential features to look for in these systems. Furthermore, compliance with international data protection standards, such as the General Data Protection Regulation (GDPR) in Europe or the California Consumer Privacy Act (CCPA) in the United States, ensures that the data handled by the AI is managed responsibly. These regulations mandate transparency in data usage, giving users confidence that their information is secure.

2. Bias in AI Models

Generative AI learns from data to generate recommendations, but the quality and fairness of its outputs depend on the data it has been trained on. If the underlying data contains biases, the AI may inadvertently replicate or amplify these biases, leading to skewed recommendations. For instance, certain deductions or tax-saving opportunities might be overlooked for specific demographics if they were underrepresented in the training data.

Addressing this requires continuous monitoring and auditing of AI models. Developers must strive to use diverse and comprehensive datasets during training and regularly update the algorithms to account for evolving tax policies and societal norms. Transparency in the model's decision-making process can also help users better understand and trust the recommendations provided.

3. The Role of Human Oversight

Generative AI is a powerful tool, but it is not infallible. Its recommendations, though data-driven, may occasionally miss nuances or fail to account for specific contexts. For example, an AI might suggest a deduction that is technically valid but not applicable to the user's unique situation due to changes in local laws or specific filing conditions.

This highlights the importance of human oversight. Financial professionals and taxpayers must critically evaluate AI-generated insights before acting on them. Combining AI's analytical power with human judgment creates a balanced approach, ensuring that tax strategies are both accurate and contextually relevant.

4. Over-Reliance on Automation

While automation is one of the most significant benefits of Generative AI, excessive dependence on these systems can lead to complacency. Users might neglect to understand the rationale behind their tax strategies, which can be problematic if unexpected issues arise. For instance, if an AI tool malfunctions or fails to incorporate recent regulatory changes, users who rely solely on its outputs may face penalties or audits.

Encouraging users to stay informed about tax basics and engage with their financial planning actively ensures a more resilient approach. Generative AI should complement, not replace, the user's involvement in their financial management.

5. Ethical Use of AI in Tax Planning

The ethical implications of Generative AI extend beyond privacy and accuracy. There is a broader question of how this technology might reinforce inequalities in access to tax benefits. High-quality AI tools often come at a cost, making them more accessible to affluent individuals and corporations than to smaller businesses or low-income taxpayers. This could widen the gap in financial efficiency and tax savings across different socio-economic groups.

Promoting equitable access to advanced tax planning tools is a responsibility that rests with developers and policymakers. Open-source AI solutions, subsidies, or partnerships with community organizations can help democratize the benefits of this technology.

Navigating the ethical and practical challenges of Generative AI in tax planning requires a multi-faceted approach. Developers must commit to transparency, fairness, and compliance in their designs, while users need to approach these tools with an informed and balanced perspective. By addressing these considerations proactively, Generative AI can serve as a reliable partner in achieving tax efficiency without compromising ethical standards or practical usability.

REAL-TIME TAX ADVICE AND COMPLIANCE

Navigating the complex world of taxes can feel overwhelming, especially with laws and regulations that change almost every year. Generative AI provides a game-changing solution by offering real-time tax advice and compliance support, making the process of managing taxes easier, faster, and far more efficient.

Tax systems around the world are governed by intricate rules that demand attention to detail. Missing deadlines, filing incorrect information, or failing to capitalize on tax benefits can lead to financial losses or even penalties. Generative AI helps individuals and businesses stay ahead of these challenges by actively monitoring financial activities, identifying tax-saving opportunities, and ensuring that all actions align with current regulations. The focus here is not just about doing taxes but doing them smarter and with greater confidence.

Understanding Real-Time Tax Advice

Generative AI has redefined the concept of real-time tax advice, offering dynamic and immediate insights that adapt to your financial activities as they happen. Unlike static tools of the past, which only offer a snapshot based on fixed data inputs, Generative AI continuously updates its recommendations, ensuring your tax strategy evolves in tandem with your financial situation. This proactive capability transforms the way individuals and businesses approach tax management, enabling smarter and faster decisions.

Imagine a scenario where you are a freelancer purchasing equipment for your work. Traditionally, you should keep receipts and manually remember to include them as deductions when filing taxes later. Generative AI simplifies this process by automatically recognizing the purchase as a deductible expense the moment it occurs. The system doesn't just flag the transaction; it categorizes it properly and highlights its impact on your overall tax strategy. This immediate assistance ensures that nothing is overlooked and minimizes the chance of missing out on valuable deductions.

What sets real-time tax advice apart is its responsiveness to changes in financial circumstances. Life rarely follows a predictable pattern, and your income, expenses, and investments can fluctuate throughout the year. Whether it's a sudden pay raise, the sale of an asset, or unexpected medical expenses, these changes can have significant tax implications. Generative AI monitors these developments in real-time and provides tailored recommendations on how to adjust your strategy. For example, if you experience a higher-than-expected income, the AI might suggest contributing to a retirement account to reduce taxable income, taking advantage of available tax deferral options.

This adaptability extends beyond just individual taxpayers. Businesses, which often face more complex financial dynamics, can use Generative AI to maintain compliance and optimize taxes across various operational activities. For instance, if a company secures a new revenue stream, the AI can immediately assess its tax implications, identifying potential deductions, credits, or adjustments that ensure the business operates within the most favorable tax parameters. This level of insight, delivered as events unfold, is invaluable for maintaining agility in a competitive marketplace.

Real-time tax advice also removes the guesswork from tax management. By integrating with your financial accounts and analyzing transactions as they occur, Generative AI can instantly evaluate whether certain actions, such as a major purchase or investment, are advantageous from a tax perspective. It can even predict the long-term consequences of these decisions. For example, if you're considering investing in a new business venture, the AI can project how this might affect your tax liability in the coming years, helping you make an informed choice before committing.

Another critical advantage of real-time advice is its ability to handle changes in tax laws. Governments frequently update tax regulations, and staying informed can be a challenge for even the most diligent taxpayers. Generative AI systems are designed to adapt swiftly, incorporating new laws into their databases as soon as they are enacted. This ensures that your tax strategy is always aligned with the latest requirements. If a new deduction or credit becomes available, the AI will flag it and explain how you can benefit. Conversely, if a change removes a benefit you've been relying on, the AI will suggest alternatives to minimize the impact.

This continuous alignment with legal standards also reduces the risk of errors or omissions that could trigger audits or penalties. Traditional methods often rely on end-of-year reviews, which can result in oversights. Generative AI, however, evaluates every transaction in real-time, ensuring that your tax filings remain accurate and compliant at all times.

The accessibility of real-time tax advice is another notable feature. These systems often come with user-friendly platforms that present insights in a clear and actionable manner. Instead of bombarding users with technical jargon, they provide simplified explanations and step-by-step guidance on implementing recommended strategies. For instance, if the AI identifies an opportunity to claim a deduction for home office expenses, it won't just flag it—it will guide you on how to calculate the appropriate amount and apply it correctly. This approach ensures that even those without extensive financial expertise can confidently manage their taxes.

Real-time advice also reduces the stress associated with tax preparation. Many taxpayers and businesses experience anxiety as tax deadlines approach, worrying about whether they've accounted for everything. Generative AI alleviates this by constantly working in the background, ensuring that all necessary information is captured and organized throughout the year. By the time filing season arrives, much of the preparation is already complete, leaving you with more time and fewer concerns.

One of the most impactful aspects of real-time tax advice is its ability to empower users with foresight. Rather than reacting to financial changes after they happen, you can proactively plan for upcoming events. For example, if you know you'll be making a significant purchase or receiving a bonus, the AI can simulate how these events will influence your tax obligations and recommend actions to optimize your position. This forward-looking capability allows you to stay ahead, turning potential tax burdens into opportunities for savings.

Staying Compliant with Evolving Regulations

Tax compliance is critical for avoiding legal trouble and financial penalties. Unfortunately, tax laws are often complex and vary significantly between countries, states, and even municipalities.

Keeping up with these changes is a daunting task, especially for businesses operating in multiple jurisdictions.

Generative AI addresses this issue by constantly updating its knowledge base with the latest tax regulations. It scans for changes in tax laws and automatically incorporates these updates into its recommendations. This means that as soon as a new regulation comes into effect, the AI ensures your financial actions comply with it.

For instance, if a government introduces a new rule requiring businesses to report certain types of transactions, Generative AI can guide you on how to adjust your reporting processes. If the rule offers a new tax credit or deduction, the AI identifies whether you qualify and calculates how to claim it. This kind of proactive compliance eliminates the risk of falling behind on legal requirements and helps you make the most of new opportunities.

Reducing Errors and Enhancing Accuracy

Mistakes in tax filings are not just frustrating—they can be costly. Errors may lead to penalties, delays in refunds, or even audits. Generative AI significantly reduces the likelihood of mistakes by automating calculations, verifying data, and ensuring accuracy in every step of the tax process.

One of the most common areas where errors occur is in data entry. For example, a business might incorrectly input expenses or overlook income from a side gig. Generative AI minimizes this risk by integrating directly with financial accounts, pulling accurate data, and cross-referencing it with tax requirements. If there's a mismatch or missing information, the system flags it for review before you file.

Additionally, AI helps ensure that all deductions and credits are correctly applied. It carefully examines your financial activities, checks for eligibility, and applies tax benefits without missing any details. By doing so, it not only prevents errors but also maximizes the value of your tax return.

Proactive Risk Management

Compliance isn't just about following the rules—it's also about managing risks. Tax authorities conduct audits to ensure accuracy and honesty in filings, and being audited can be a stressful experience. Generative AI can help you prepare for audits by keeping detailed, organized records of your financial transactions and ensuring your filings are error-free.

The AI also analyzes patterns in your financial data to identify any potential red flags that could trigger an audit. For example, if your expense claims seem unusually high compared to your income, the system might suggest reducing certain deductions or providing additional documentation to justify them. This kind of proactive risk management not only keeps you compliant but also gives you peace of mind knowing that your taxes are audit-ready.

Real-Time Monitoring of Financial Activities

Another powerful feature of Generative AI is its ability to monitor your financial activities in real time. As you earn, spend, and save, the AI continually tracks these transactions, categorizes them, and evaluates their impact on your tax situation.

For instance, if you make a significant purchase, the AI immediately determines whether it qualifies as a deductible expense. If you receive income from multiple sources, such as a main job and freelance work, the AI calculates how much tax you owe on each income stream and suggests strategies to minimize the total amount. This ongoing monitoring means that you're always aware of your tax obligations and opportunities, reducing the chance of surprises when it's time to file.

Streamlining Tax Filing Processes

Tax filing has traditionally been seen as a labor-intensive and often stressful task. However, the integration of Generative AI into this process brings an unprecedented level of ease and efficiency. Unlike manual methods, which require individuals to sort through financial records and interpret complex tax laws, AI-powered systems handle these tasks with remarkable accuracy and speed.

At its core, Generative AI transforms tax filing into a seamless experience by automating critical steps. It starts by collecting and categorizing financial data, ensuring that every piece of relevant information is accounted for. This eliminates the common issue of missing receipts or overlooking income sources. The AI ensures that all numbers are accurate and organized, laying a solid foundation for precise tax calculations.

A particularly beneficial feature is the AI's ability to interpret tax forms. These documents often contain technical language that can confuse even seasoned taxpayers. Generative AI deciphers these forms and translates them into simple, actionable steps. For instance, if a particular section requires details about deductions, the AI identifies the relevant expenses from your financial data and fills in the form accordingly. This functionality is invaluable for individuals unfamiliar with tax jargon, as it removes guesswork and reduces the risk of errors.

Generative AI also addresses the challenge of ensuring compliance with deadlines. Taxpayers often struggle to keep track of when filings are due, especially if they have multiple income sources or operate in various regions. AI systems proactively send reminders well in advance, giving users ample time to prepare. Additionally, they can automatically submit completed forms directly to tax authorities, bypassing the need for manual uploads or mailings.

For businesses, the advantages are even more pronounced. Generative AI integrates seamlessly with accounting software, pulling data directly from systems used to manage payroll, inventory, and expenses. This integration streamlines the preparation of more complex filings, such as those involving corporate taxes or VAT. By handling large datasets effortlessly, the AI minimizes the burden on financial teams, allowing them to focus on strategic planning rather than administrative tasks.

One of the standout benefits of using Generative AI for tax filing is its ability to adapt to changes in tax laws. Regulations frequently evolve, and staying updated can be daunting. AI systems are programmed to learn these changes in real time, ensuring that filings adhere to the latest requirements. This not only prevents penalties for non-compliance but also helps users capitalize on new deductions or credits that they might otherwise overlook.

Beyond accuracy and compliance, Generative AI introduces an element of personalization into the tax filing process. It evaluates individual financial situations and offers tailored recommendations for optimizing tax outcomes. For example, if you're eligible for deductions related to charitable donations or energy-efficient home upgrades, the AI highlights these opportunities and incorporates them into your filing. This level of customization ensures that every user maximizes their tax savings without unnecessary effort.

The convenience of AI-driven tax filing extends to its user-friendly interfaces. Many systems are designed with intuitive dashboards that guide users through the process step by step. These platforms often include features like interactive help tools or virtual assistants that answer questions in real time. For individuals who are not tech-savvy, these features make adopting AI solutions straightforward and accessible.

Generative AI doesn't just simplify filing; it transforms it into a proactive process. Instead of waiting until tax season to gather information, the AI monitors financial activity throughout the year, identifying potential deductions as they occur. This ongoing analysis means that when it's time to file, much of the groundwork has already been completed. As a result, the entire process takes significantly less time and effort.

Generative AI enhances the overall user experience by providing peace of mind. Knowing that your taxes are filed accurately and on time eliminates a major source of stress. Whether you're an individual taxpayer or a business owner, the confidence that comes from using a reliable, advanced system is invaluable. The streamlined, intelligent approach of Generative AI ensures that tax filing is no longer a dreaded chore but an efficient and manageable task.

Empowering Small Businesses and Freelancers

Small businesses and freelancers represent a dynamic but often under-resourced segment of the economy. Tax management can be particularly burdensome for these groups, as they frequently deal with fluctuating income, complex deductions, and limited access to professional financial services. Generative AI steps in as a powerful solution, addressing these unique challenges with tailored, cost-effective, and user-friendly tools.

For small businesses, managing taxes involves more than just filing returns—it's about navigating payroll taxes, sales tax obligations, and potential deductions across diverse operational activities. These businesses often lack dedicated accounting teams, relying instead on manual processes or generalized software that may not cater to their specific needs. Generative AI transforms this landscape by integrating seamlessly into business workflows, automatically tracking financial data, and identifying tax-saving opportunities.

Imagine a local café owner juggling multiple responsibilities, from managing employees to sourcing inventory. Generative AI simplifies their tax obligations by automatically categorizing transactions, such as expenses for raw materials or wages paid to staff. It provides real-time updates on how these expenses impact their overall tax liability, ensuring nothing is missed when it's time to file. Additionally, the system can track sales tax requirements for products sold in different jurisdictions, a particularly challenging task for businesses with an online presence.

Freelancers face their own set of hurdles, particularly when it comes to irregular income and quarterly estimated tax payments. Without a steady paycheck or employer withholding taxes on their behalf, freelancers must calculate and remit payments to tax authorities themselves. This process can be daunting, especially for those new to self-employment. Generative AI simplifies it by analyzing income patterns and calculating the precise amount owed each quarter. By providing reminders and even generating the necessary forms, it reduces the risk of underpayment penalties and helps freelancers stay on top of their obligations.

Another challenge for freelancers is identifying deductions that apply to their work. Many self-employed individuals miss out on valuable tax breaks because they aren't aware of what qualifies. Generative AI changes this by scanning financial transactions and automatically flagging deductible expenses. For instance, if a freelance graphic designer purchases a new laptop, the AI recognizes it as a business expense and determines how it can be depreciated for tax purposes. Similarly, home office expenses, professional memberships, and even a portion of utilities can be categorized and claimed with precision.

Generative AI also addresses the need for documentation, a critical aspect of tax compliance for both freelancers and small businesses. Keeping organized records of income and expenses is essential not only for accurate filings but also in the event of an audit. The AI system automates this process by securely storing digital copies of receipts, invoices, and financial statements. It creates an accessible archive that users can reference anytime, ensuring they're always prepared for inquiries from tax authorities.

The adaptability of Generative AI makes it especially valuable for small businesses and freelancers working in rapidly changing environments. For instance, during the COVID-19 pandemic, many governments introduced new tax credits and relief programs to support struggling businesses. Understanding and applying for these benefits was a significant challenge for many. Generative AI, equipped with real-time updates and contextual understanding, could identify eligibility for relief measures and guide users through the application process. This responsiveness not only saved time but also ensured that businesses and freelancers received the support they were entitled to.

One of the most compelling aspects of Generative AI is its affordability. Hiring a professional accountant or tax consultant can be prohibitively expensive for many small operations, especially those just starting out. By providing comparable expertise at a fraction of the cost, AI democratizes access to sophisticated tax management tools. This allows even the smallest businesses and independent professionals to operate with the confidence and efficiency of larger organizations.

For small businesses expanding into e-commerce, tax compliance becomes even more intricate. Selling products across state or national borders introduces a web of sales tax regulations that vary by location. Generative AI excels in this context by tracking where sales are made and ensuring that the correct taxes are applied and remitted. This capability is crucial for businesses looking to scale without being bogged down by administrative complexities.

Freelancers working internationally also benefit from Generative AI's ability to navigate cross-border tax issues. Income earned from clients in different countries may be subject to varying tax treaties or withholding requirements. The AI can analyze these situations and provide guidance on how to report income correctly while minimizing unnecessary tax burdens. This global perspective is particularly valuable for digital freelancers, such as writers, designers, or developers, who often collaborate with clients worldwide.

Another strength of Generative AI lies in its ability to educate users. For many small business owners and freelancers, taxes are not just a task to be completed—they're a source of confusion and anxiety. Generative AI bridges this gap by not only performing calculations but also explaining the reasoning behind them in plain language. This empowers users to understand their financial situation more deeply, fostering better decision-making and long-term financial health.

For example, a photographer who spends heavily on equipment and travel might struggle to balance their expenses with tax obligations. Generative AI can break down these costs, showing how they reduce taxable income while providing recommendations on how to optimize spending for future tax advantages. This kind of tailored advice helps freelancers and small businesses make informed choices that benefit them both financially and operationally.

As technology advances, the role of Generative AI in supporting small businesses and freelancers will only grow. Future developments may include enhanced forecasting capabilities, allowing users to simulate how different financial scenarios could impact their taxes. For instance, a small business considering hiring an additional employee could use AI to calculate how this decision would affect payroll taxes, deductions, and overall profitability.

A Global Perspective on Tax Compliance

For businesses operating internationally, tax compliance becomes even more complicated. Each country has its own tax codes, reporting requirements, and deadlines. Generative AI helps manage this complexity by offering a global perspective on tax compliance. By integrating data from multiple jurisdictions, the AI ensures that businesses meet all local requirements while minimizing their overall tax burden. It identifies opportunities to leverage international tax treaties, avoid double taxation, and optimize cross-border transactions. This capability is especially valuable for multinational corporations, but it can also benefit small businesses expanding into global markets.

Future Innovations in Tax Advice

As Generative AI technology continues to evolve, its capabilities in tax advice and compliance will only improve. Future innovations may include even more personalized guidance based on individual financial goals, seamless integration with blockchain for secure data storage, and enhanced collaboration with tax authorities to simplify compliance further.

Imagine a future where your AI assistant not only manages your taxes but also helps you plan for major financial milestones, such as buying a home or starting a business, with full consideration of tax implications. This level of integration would make financial management more holistic and effective than ever before.

Case Studies on Tax Efficiency Using Generative AI Tools

Generative AI has revolutionized the way taxes are approached, offering innovative solutions that streamline complex financial processes. By applying advanced algorithms to tax planning, individuals and organizations can uncover new opportunities for savings, improve compliance with regulations, and significantly reduce administrative burdens. Its capability to analyze vast amounts of financial data and generate tailored strategies ensures that even the most intricate tax scenarios are addressed with precision.

Through practical examples, the transformative impact of

this technology becomes evident, illustrating its ability to adapt to diverse needs. Whether optimizing deductions for a small business, simplifying tax filing for freelancers, or enhancing compliance for multinational corporations, Generative AI introduces a level of efficiency and accuracy that was previously unattainable. These examples serve as valuable lessons, providing actionable insights that empower users to adopt smarter, more effective tax strategies tailored to their unique circumstances.

Case Study: A Small Business Discovers Tax Savings

A local bakery had been struggling with increasing operational costs and tighter profit margins. The business owner, who managed all financial tasks alone, often overlooked deductions and failed to utilize the tax breaks available to small businesses fully. Overwhelmed by the complexity of the tax code, they decided to try a Generative AI tax tool recommended by a colleague.

The AI solution immediately began analyzing the bakery's financial records, including purchase receipts, payroll data, and utility bills. It flagged several missed deductions, such as equipment depreciation, business meals, and vehicle expenses for deliveries. Additionally, the tool identified a tax credit for hiring employees from underserved communities, something the owner hadn't been aware of. Within weeks, the bakery had an entirely updated tax strategy.

By the end of the fiscal year, the bakery reported a 25% reduction in taxable income, which translated into significant savings. Beyond just saving money, the AI tool provided real-time recommendations for managing expenses more strategically throughout the year. The owner described the experience as "like having a personal financial advisor, but without the cost."

Case Study: Freelancers Gaining Clarity in Tax Filing

Freelancers often face challenges in managing taxes due to the irregular nature of their income and the variety of deductions applicable to their work. For a graphic designer juggling multiple projects and income streams, filing taxes had always been a stressful and time-consuming process. Traditional tax software offered limited support, often missing key deductions tied to their work-from-home setup.

Upon integrating a Generative AI-powered tax tool, the designer experienced a drastic shift. The AI system scanned emails for payment confirmations, categorized business expenses such as design software subscriptions and client travel, and even flagged costs like home internet usage that could be partially claimed. It also recommended establishing a dedicated home office to maximize deductions further.

Perhaps the most valuable feature was the tool's predictive capabilities. It suggested quarterly tax payments based on projected earnings, reducing the burden of an annual lump sum and avoiding penalties for underpayment. By the end of the tax season, the freelancer saved 18% on taxes compared to previous years and gained a better understanding of how to manage finances moving forward.

Case Study: A Non-Profit Navigates Complex Tax Codes

Non-profit organizations operate under unique tax rules, requiring them to file specific forms and adhere to strict regulations. One regional charity faced difficulty maintaining compliance due to staff shortages and the complexity of its tax obligations. Manual record-keeping left room for errors, and potential penalties loomed large.

The charity decided to invest in a Generative AI-based tax compliance tool designed for non-profits. This system quickly digitized years of paper records and identified discrepancies in prior filings. More importantly, it highlighted underutilized exemptions and credits for non-profits, including those for energy-efficient upgrades to their facility.

Additionally, the AI tool introduced a structured workflow, reminding the team about important filing deadlines and alerting them to new regulations that could affect their compliance. Within six months, the charity had not only resolved past issues but also improved its financial planning process. Staff reported feeling less overwhelmed, and donors appreciated the increased transparency in financial reporting.

Case Study: Corporate Tax Efficiency Across Borders

A multinational corporation with operations in five countries faced challenges in managing taxes across multiple jurisdictions. Different regulations, exchange rates, and compliance requirements created a significant administrative burden, increasing the risk of penalties. The finance team needed a robust solution to harmonize global tax practices while identifying potential savings.

The company adopted a Generative AI platform tailored for multinational operations. This tool analyzed tax treaties between countries to optimize transfer pricing, minimizing the risk of double taxation on cross-border transactions. Additionally, it flagged inconsistencies in value-added tax (VAT) filings, helping the company recover significant amounts in refunds.

One notable achievement was the identification of regional tax incentives for green initiatives. By transitioning to renewable energy sources at its manufacturing plants, the corporation not only reduced operational costs but also qualified for substantial tax credits. The AI system also generated detailed compliance reports that streamlined the auditing process, ensuring transparency with regulators in each jurisdiction.

Within a year, the corporation reported savings of millions

of dollars in tax liabilities and a marked improvement in compliance ratings globally. The CFO described the AI system as "indispensable in navigating the complexities of modern taxation."

Case Study: Simplifying Tax Planning for Retirees

Retirees often face unique tax challenges, especially when managing multiple income sources like pensions, social security, and investment returns. For one couple nearing retirement, financial planning became a daunting task. Their accountant struggled to provide proactive advice, and they worried about outliving their savings.

At the recommendation of their financial advisor, they tried a Generative AI-based tax optimization tool. The AI immediately created a comprehensive analysis of their financial situation, suggesting strategies such as withdrawing funds from retirement accounts in tax-efficient increments and delaying social security benefits for maximum payouts.

The tool also identified ways to minimize capital gains taxes by restructuring the investment portfolio. By prioritizing tax-advantaged accounts for high-growth assets, the couple reduced their tax burden significantly. Additionally, it flagged opportunities for charitable giving that not only aligned with their values but also provided substantial tax benefits.

For the couple, the AI tool offered peace of mind, helping them navigate retirement with greater confidence. They reported feeling more secure in their financial future, thanks to the detailed guidance and proactive alerts provided by the system.

Lessons Learned from These Case Studies

The real-world examples above demonstrate the versatility and effectiveness of Generative AI in tax optimization. Here are some key takeaways from these scenarios:

- Personalization is Key: Generative AI excels in tailoring tax strategies to individual circumstances, ensuring that unique needs and goals are met.
- Real-Time Adaptation: The ability to update recommendations based on current financial data makes AI tools invaluable in dynamic environments.
- Error Reduction: By automating calculations and identifying potential discrepancies, AI significantly reduces the risk of costly mistakes.
- Efficiency Gains: Businesses and individuals alike save time and resources by letting AI handle complex tax scenarios, freeing them to focus on other priorities.

Beyond Efficiency: The Broader Impact of Generative AI on Taxation

While these case studies highlight immediate financial benefits, the broader implications of Generative AI extend beyond individual savings. By simplifying tax compliance and uncovering opportunities for optimization, AI tools contribute to a fairer, more transparent financial system. Governments and regulators can also leverage these technologies to improve efficiency and reduce fraud.

The integration of Generative AI into tax practices marks a pivotal moment in financial innovation, offering transformative possibilities for users at all levels.

CHAPTER 7

LONG-TERM FINANCIAL PLANNING

Long-term financial planning is essential for creating a life of stability and opportunity. It extends far beyond simply saving money; it encompasses designing a financial roadmap to prepare for both anticipated and unforeseen events. Whether planning for retirement, securing your family's future, or funding major life goals like education, long-term financial planning ensures you are ready for life's financial challenges. However, traditional methods often struggle to address the dynamic and interconnected nature of these needs.

Generative AI offers a groundbreaking approach by leveraging data-driven insights to simplify and enhance this intricate process. Unlike conventional tools, which rely on static calculations or generic advice, Generative AI can analyze real-time data, predict future trends, and generate personalized strategies that evolve with your circumstances. It learns from your financial behavior, adapts to changing market conditions, and creates solutions tailored specifically for you.

For instance, when planning for retirement, Generative AI doesn't just calculate how much you need to save—it factors in variables like inflation, fluctuating expenses, and shifting market trends to build a comprehensive, adaptable strategy. Similarly, in estate planning, it can optimize how assets are allocated to reduce taxes and ensure your family's financial security.

The transformative power of Generative AI lies in its ability to make complex decisions feel manageable. It acts as a virtual financial advisor, capable of providing insights that are not only accurate but also deeply personalized. By addressing long-term goals such as retirement, family milestones, and wealth transfer, Generative AI turns financial planning into a proactive and informed process. This empowers individuals to not just react to financial demands but to anticipate and prepare for them confidently, building a future that aligns with their aspirations.

AI IN RETIREMENT PLANNING

Retirement planning is no longer about guesswork or relying solely on generic financial advice. Generative AI allows individuals to plan for retirement with precision, taking into account factors like income changes, market trends, and personal goals. It provides actionable insights that ensure a comfortable retirement while adapting to unexpected challenges.

Generative AI works by analyzing vast amounts of financial data, including market conditions, spending habits, and potential risks. It then generates projections that can guide your financial decisions. For example, if you aim to retire by 60, Generative AI can calculate how much you need to save annually based on your income, expenses, and desired lifestyle. Unlike traditional tools, it dynamically adjusts these calculations as your financial situation changes.

One of the standout features of Generative AI is its ability to simulate different market scenarios. It doesn't just tell you how much to save—it shows you what happens to your investments during market booms, recessions, or even unexpected global events. This enables you to plan for various possibilities, ensuring you are prepared no matter what happens.

Additionally, Generative AI can recommend the best ways to withdraw money during retirement to maximize your savings. It ensures that you can maintain your lifestyle while protecting your funds. For instance, if you have multiple retirement accounts, AI can suggest which one to draw from first to minimize taxes or preserve funds for future use.

PERSONALIZED RETIREMENT GOALS

Generative AI transforms retirement planning by providing strategies that are as unique as the individuals using them. Unlike traditional methods that rely on generalized assumptions, Generative AI digs deep into your financial habits, aspirations, and potential challenges to craft a customized plan. This adaptability ensures that your retirement strategy evolves alongside your circumstances, helping you meet your goals without compromising your lifestyle.

For example, if your vision of retirement includes frequent travel, Generative AI can account for these additional expenses in your savings plan. It will predict future travel costs, including inflation and currency fluctuations, and adjust your investment strategies to ensure adequate funds are available. Similarly, if you anticipate healthcare needs during retirement, the AI incorporates these potential expenses into your financial projections, recommending specific savings or insurance solutions to address them.

Beyond meeting specific goals, Generative AI excels at balancing competing priorities. Consider a family managing dual incomes while covering education costs for children and mortgage payments. Generative AI can analyze their cash flow to determine how much they can realistically save for retirement without jeopardizing current obligations. It dynamically adjusts contributions based on changes like salary increases, unexpected expenses, or financial windfalls, ensuring retirement savings remain on track.

Moreover, Generative AI brings foresight into the planning process. It predicts the financial impact of decisions made today on your retirement years. For instance, if a family considers upgrading their home, the AI can estimate how that investment affects their long-term savings goals, helping them make informed choices. This proactive approach eliminates guesswork, enabling individuals to pursue their ideal retirement confidently.

By tailoring plans to reflect personal circumstances and adjusting them as life unfolds, Generative AI makes retirement planning not just effective but truly relevant to individual needs and aspirations.

ESTATE PLANNING MADE SIMPLE

Estate planning often feels complicated and overwhelming, but Generative AI makes it much more manageable. Estate planning involves organizing your assets and determining how they will be distributed after your lifetime. This process ensures that your loved ones are cared for and that your wishes are honored. Generative AI simplifies this process by offering tools that guide you through each step.

Generative AI can help identify the most tax-efficient ways to distribute your assets. For instance, it might suggest transferring certain assets into a trust to reduce tax liabilities for your heirs. The AI can also recommend strategies to avoid common pitfalls, like not updating your estate plan after a major life event such as marriage, divorce, or the birth of a child.

Additionally, Generative AI ensures your estate plan aligns with current legal and regulatory requirements. It stays updated on changes to tax laws or inheritance regulations, so you don't have to worry about compliance. This is especially useful for people with assets in multiple countries, where laws can vary significantly.

Another benefit of using Generative AI in estate planning is its ability to provide clear, actionable insights. For example, if you want to leave a portion of your wealth to charity, AI can help you choose the most effective way to do so, whether through a charitable trust or a donor-advised fund. It simplifies these decisions by presenting the pros and cons of each option in an easy-to-understand way.

PLANNING FOR MAJOR LIFE EVENTS

Financial planning is not just about retirement or inheritance; it's also about navigating the financial demands of major life events. Generative AI helps individuals and families prepare for these milestones with confidence and clarity.

Marriage and Parenthood

When planning for marriage, AI can help couples create joint financial plans that accommodate shared goals. It can identify potential areas of conflict, like differing spending habits, and suggest strategies to address them. For parents, Generative AI provides tools to estimate future expenses for raising a child, including education costs, extracurricular activities, and healthcare. For example, a couple planning to have a child in five years can use Generative AI to predict how much they'll need to save annually to cover daycare and schooling expenses. The AI adapts these predictions as circumstances change, such as a career promotion or an unexpected expense.

Education Planning

Education is one of the most significant investments parents make for their children. Generative AI simplifies this process by providing accurate cost forecasts and savings strategies. It considers factors like inflation, tuition increases, and the availability of scholarships or grants.

For instance, if you want your child to attend a private university, Generative AI can calculate how much you need to save monthly to meet that goal. It can also suggest the best financial instruments, like education savings plans, to maximize your contributions.

BUILDING GENERATIONAL WEALTH

Generative AI goes beyond addressing short-term financial goals; it is a powerful tool for creating and sustaining wealth that can benefit future generations. By offering insights into wealth-building strategies and preserving assets, it enables families to secure long-term financial stability while fostering opportunities for their heirs.

A key advantage of Generative AI in generational wealth planning is its ability to create well-balanced investment portfolios. These portfolios are designed to minimize risk while maximizing growth, taking into account factors such as market volatility, economic trends, and the family's financial goals. By constantly analyzing financial data and projecting future market scenarios, AI ensures that investments remain on track to deliver steady returns over time.

Generative AI also identifies opportunities for wealth transfer that can reduce tax burdens while maintaining the integrity of a financial legacy. For example, it can suggest tax-efficient ways to gift assets to children or grandchildren during your lifetime, such as annual gifting limits that avoid triggering taxes. This proactive approach ensures that wealth is passed down smoothly and with minimal financial loss.

In addition to managing individual assets, Generative AI is particularly effective at creating collective financial plans for families spanning multiple generations. Set up family trusts or endowments to pool and manage resources responsibly. These structures not only protect wealth but also align with the family's values and goals, such as funding education, supporting philanthropic efforts, or investing in business ventures that benefit future generations.

Generative AI's predictive capabilities also help families anticipate challenges that could affect their financial legacy. For instance, it can highlight potential risks such as changing inheritance laws, economic downturns, or shifts in family dynamics that might require adjustments to the plan. By addressing these challenges early, families can avoid disruptions and safeguard their financial stability.

Moreover, Generative AI fosters financial literacy and collaboration within families. It provides tools and insights that encourage open communication about financial goals, ensuring that each member understands their role in preserving and growing the family's wealth. This shared understanding helps create a cohesive strategy that aligns individual aspirations with collective priorities.

By offering tailored solutions for wealth management, preservation, and transfer, Generative AI ensures that financial security is not only achieved for the present but also sustained for future generations. This forward-looking approach empowers families to build a lasting legacy that reflects their values and provides a foundation for success.

CHALLENGES AND ETHICAL CONSIDERATIONS

Generative AI provides transformative benefits, but it is vital to understand the challenges and ethical implications associated with its use. One significant issue is ensuring data privacy. Since Generative AI processes sensitive financial information to generate insights, safeguarding this data against breaches or unauthorized access becomes critical. Organizations must implement robust encryption methods, secure storage systems, and strict access controls to protect user data. Individuals also need to remain vigilant about how and where their financial data is shared.

Another concern arises from bias in the data that trains Generative AI models. Historical financial datasets can reflect inequities or discriminatory practices. For example, if a dataset prioritizes higher-income earners or particular demographics, the AI might unintentionally favor similar groups in its recommendations. This can result in unfair outcomes, such as providing less accurate predictions or fewer options to underrepresented groups. To address this, developers need to ensure diverse and inclusive training data while regularly evaluating and refining the algorithms to detect and eliminate biases.

Transparency in decision-making is another ethical priority. Generative AI often operates as a "black box," making decisions based on complex computations that may not be easily understood. Users should have access to clear explanations about how conclusions are reached. For example, if an AI suggests changes to a retirement savings plan, it should explain the reasoning behind its recommendations in simple, accessible terms.

While Generative AI is a powerful tool, it cannot replace the nuanced judgment of human financial advisors or planners. Life circumstances, emotional factors, and unique family dynamics often require empathy and contextual understanding that AI lacks. For instance, while AI may recommend aggressive investment strategies for higher returns, a human advisor might recognize the individual's comfort level with risk and adjust the plan accordingly.

Generative AI must be seen as a complementary tool that enhances human decision-making rather than replacing it. By acknowledging its limitations and integrating ethical safeguards, users can benefit from the technology while mitigating risks. A balanced approach ensures that Generative AI remains a reliable and equitable resource for long-term financial planning.

AI IN RETIREMENT PLANNING

Retirement planning stands as a cornerstone of financial stability, demanding foresight, disciplined saving habits, and effective investment strategies. It ensures individuals can transition into a phase of life without the financial pressures tied to active income. However, the unpredictability of economic factors such as market volatility, inflation trends, and life's unexpected events often complicate this process, leaving many feeling uncertain about their financial readiness.

Generative AI emerges as a transformative solution to these challenges, reshaping how individuals approach retirement preparation. Unlike traditional methods that rely on generalized projections or static financial advice, this technology leverages vast datasets to deliver deeply personalized and forward-looking insights. By integrating real-time analytics and predictive modeling, Generative AI adapts to changes in individual circumstances and the broader economic landscape, ensuring tailored, actionable plans for retirement success.

Through its ability to synthesize complex data and provide precise recommendations, Generative AI equips users with the tools to navigate these uncertainties with confidence. It doesn't merely simplify retirement planning—it redefines it, making the process more efficient, adaptable, and aligned with personal aspirations.

Transforming Retirement Planning with Generative AI

Generative AI revolutionizes the way people approach retirement planning. Unlike traditional methods that rely on static projections and fixed strategies, Generative AI adapts to real-time data and personal circumstances, offering tailored solutions. It uses advanced models to analyze patterns, forecast trends, and suggest actionable steps to help individuals achieve their financial goals.

Imagine having a tool that continuously monitors your income, expenses, and investments, adjusting your retirement plan as your financial situation evolves. This dynamic approach ensures that your plan remains relevant, even as life changes.

Customized Retirement Goals

Generative AI provides a highly personalized approach to retirement planning, enabling individuals to turn their unique aspirations into actionable financial strategies. Whether the goal is to explore exotic destinations, launch a passion project, or lead a simple, stress-free retirement, this technology offers a clear path forward. By delving into the nuances of an individual's financial habits, income streams, and long-term objectives, AI generates customized roadmaps that align resources with these ambitions.

For instance, someone with a consistent salary but limited savings might find it challenging to secure a financially stable retirement. Here, Generative AI steps in to uncover spending habits that hinder progress and suggest smarter saving methods. These insights may include reallocating funds from less impactful expenditures or recommending high-growth savings vehicles tailored to their financial profile. This level of personalization ensures that each recommendation is specific to the user's situation, providing a practical and efficient way to bridge the gap between their current financial standing and their future goals.

What sets Generative AI apart is its adaptability. As life circumstances evolve, such as changes in income, family dynamics, or financial priorities, the technology recalibrates the retirement strategy, keeping it relevant and effective. This dynamic feature makes it not just a planning tool but a financial companion capable of guiding users toward a secure and fulfilling retirement.

Simulating Market Scenarios

The financial markets are unpredictable, and investment decisions made today can significantly impact retirement funds years down the line. Generative AI helps mitigate these uncertainties by simulating various market scenarios. It uses historical data and predictive algorithms to model potential outcomes, giving individuals a clearer picture of how different investment strategies might perform over time.

For instance, if a person is considering investing in stocks versus bonds for their retirement portfolio, AI can generate multiple scenarios to show how each option might fare under different economic conditions. This allows individuals to make informed choices, balancing risk and reward according to their comfort levels.

Real-Time Adjustments

One of the standout features of Generative AI in retirement planning is its ability to provide real-time adjustments. Life is rarely predictable—unexpected expenses, career changes, or economic downturns can all disrupt a well-laid retirement plan. Generative AI constantly monitors these changes and recalibrates the plan to keep it on track.

Consider a scenario where an individual receives a significant bonus or inherits some money. Generative AI can quickly integrate this new income into the retirement plan, suggesting the best ways to allocate it—whether that's increasing contributions to a retirement account, paying off debt, or investing in high-yield opportunities. Similarly, if someone loses a job or faces a financial emergency, the tool can recommend adjustments to spending and saving patterns to minimize the impact on long-term goals.

Sustainable Withdrawal Strategies

A critical aspect of retirement planning is deciding how to withdraw funds once you've retired. Taking out too much money too quickly can deplete savings, while being overly cautious can result in an unnecessarily frugal lifestyle. Generative AI helps strike the right balance by creating sustainable withdrawal strategies. These strategies take into account factors like life expectancy, healthcare costs, and market performance. For example, AI might recommend withdrawing a specific percentage of savings annually, adjusting the amount based on inflation and investment returns. This ensures that retirees can maintain their desired lifestyle without risking financial insecurity.

Adapting to Changing Circumstances

Retirement planning isn't a one-time event—it's a lifelong process that evolves as circumstances change. Generative AI excels in adapting to these changes, ensuring that the retirement plan remains effective throughout life. For example, as individuals age, their risk tolerance often decreases. AI can identify this shift and suggest moving investments from high-risk assets like stocks to more stable options like bonds or fixed-income funds. Similarly, healthcare is a major consideration in retirement. Generative AI can predict potential medical expenses based on factors like family history and lifestyle, incorporating these costs into the overall plan. This proactive approach helps individuals avoid being blindsided by unexpected expenses.

Case Study: Adapting Retirement Plans in Real Time

Consider a 45-year-old professional who has been saving diligently for retirement. Over the years, they've contributed to a retirement account, invested in a mix of stocks and mutual funds, and maintained a modest lifestyle. However, an unexpected economic downturn leads to significant losses in their investment portfolio.

With the help of Generative AI, the individual's retirement plan is quickly adjusted. The AI tool analyzes the market conditions, recommends reallocating investments to less volatile assets, and suggests temporarily increasing contributions to the retirement account to compensate for the losses. Within a few months, the individual's financial trajectory is back on track, demonstrating the resilience and adaptability of AI-driven planning.

Maximizing Tax Efficiency

Generative AI also plays a crucial role in optimizing the tax aspects of retirement planning. Taxes can significantly impact the amount of money available during retirement, but AI can identify strategies to minimize this burden. For instance, it might suggest contributing to tax-advantaged accounts like 401(k)s or IRAs, or it could recommend timing withdrawals in a way that reduces taxable income.

Additionally, AI can help retirees navigate complex tax laws that vary by state or country. By staying updated on the latest regulations, individuals ensure that they remain compliant while maximizing their financial benefits.

Making Retirement Accessible to Everyone

Generative AI has the transformative ability to make retirement planning a universal tool, accessible to individuals from all economic backgrounds. Historically, personalized financial planning was reserved for those who could afford expensive financial advisors, leaving a significant portion of the population without adequate guidance. Generative AI changes this narrative by offering affordable, efficient, and highly personalized solutions, breaking down the traditional barriers to entry.

For young professionals who may feel overwhelmed by the complexities of saving for retirement early in their careers, Generative AI simplifies the process. It provides actionable insights tailored to their income levels, spending habits, and long-term goals, turning an intimidating task into a manageable and achievable plan. Meanwhile, midlife savers who feel they are behind on their retirement goals can use AI-driven strategies to make up for lost time. The technology identifies opportunities for catch-up contributions, suggests efficient savings vehicles, and recalibrates plans to meet tighter timelines.

By reducing reliance on high-cost services, Generative AI levels the playing field. Its tools require minimal user expertise, providing intuitive interfaces and step-by-step guidance. This means that even individuals with limited financial literacy can create and maintain a robust retirement plan. Moreover, the scalability of AI-driven solutions allows for widespread adoption, ensuring that personalized retirement advice is no longer a privilege but a standard offering for anyone seeking financial security.

Generative AI doesn't just address financial disparities—it actively works to close them. By offering accessible, inclusive, and effective planning tools, it empowers individuals to take charge of their retirement futures, regardless of their starting point. This democratization of retirement planning represents a major shift toward financial equity, making long-term security a reality for all.

Ethical Considerations in AI-Driven Retirement Planning

As Generative AI becomes an integral part of retirement planning, it is essential to address the ethical challenges that accompany its widespread use. One of the primary concerns is the protection of user data. Financial details are among the most sensitive pieces of personal information, and their misuse or exposure can lead to significant risks, including identity theft or financial fraud. Ensuring that AI platforms prioritize robust security measures, such as encryption and secure data storage, is critical to maintaining user trust.

Another major ethical issue lies in the potential for bias within

AI systems. Since Generative AI models learn from historical data, they can inadvertently replicate and reinforce existing inequalities or inaccuracies present in their training datasets. For example, if a dataset contains biases favoring certain socioeconomic groups, the AI may generate recommendations that inadvertently disadvantage underrepresented populations. To mitigate this, developers must continually audit and refine AI models, ensuring that their outputs are fair, equitable, and reflective of diverse perspectives.

Transparency is also a key consideration. Users need to understand how AI reaches its conclusions and recommendations. Without clear explanations of the algorithms' decision-making processes, individuals may struggle to trust or act on the insights provided. Building systems that clearly communicate the rationale behind their outputs can empower users and foster greater confidence in the technology.

Regulatory compliance plays a crucial role in ensuring the ethical deployment of Generative AI in retirement planning. Governments and industry bodies must establish guidelines to protect users from potential exploitation or misuse of AI tools. Developers and financial planners leveraging AI must stay informed of these regulations to ensure their practices are both ethical and legally compliant.

Incorporating these considerations into the development and use of Generative AI tools is essential to harness their full potential while safeguarding the interests of all users. Ethical practices not only enhance trust but also pave the way for more inclusive and effective financial planning solutions.

ESTATE PLANNING AND LIFECYCLE FINANCIAL PLANNING

Estate planning and lifecycle financial planning are essential components of long-term financial security. Together, they ensure that your wealth is effectively managed, protected, and distributed throughout your life and beyond. Generative AI introduces a transformative approach to these complex processes, providing tailored strategies that adapt to changing circumstances and personal goals. By leveraging the predictive power of AI, individuals and families can confidently navigate financial uncertainties, secure their legacy, and maintain stability across different life stages.

Estate Planning Simplified with Generative AI

Estate planning is the process of organizing and managing your assets to ensure they are distributed according to your wishes after your passing. While traditionally a task requiring extensive legal and financial expertise, Generative AI has made estate planning more accessible and efficient. This technology provides personalized solutions by analyzing your financial situation, family dynamics, and long-term objectives.

One of the primary benefits of Generative AI in estate planning is its ability to create customized plans that are both comprehensive and flexible. For instance, it can analyze your current assets, forecast potential growth or depreciation, and recommend strategies to maximize their value. Whether it's property, investments, or savings, AI helps ensure that your wealth is distributed in a way that aligns with your values and the needs of your beneficiaries.

A common challenge in estate planning is ensuring that your assets are protected from unnecessary taxation. Generative AI excels in identifying opportunities to minimize taxes by suggesting options like trusts, charitable contributions, or gifting strategies. By doing so, it not only preserves the value of your estate but also ensures that your family or chosen beneficiaries receive the maximum benefit.

Furthermore, Generative AI simplifies the legal aspects of estate planning. It can assist in drafting wills, powers of attorney, and other essential documents. While these outputs should always be reviewed by a qualified legal professional, the initial groundwork done by AI reduces the time and cost involved in the planning process. For instance, if you want to set up a trust for a minor child, AI can recommend the best type of trust based on your goals and the child's needs.

Another important aspect of estate planning is the fair distribution of assets. Generative AI takes into account family dynamics and preferences to create equitable solutions. For instance, if you own multiple properties or investments, the system can suggest ways to divide them among beneficiaries that minimize potential conflicts. This helps maintain harmony within families while respecting your wishes.

Generative AI also provides ongoing support by adapting your estate plan as your circumstances change. Life is unpredictable, and your financial situation or family dynamics may evolve over time. AI continuously monitors these changes and offers updated recommendations. For example, if you acquire new assets or if tax laws shift, AI will revise your plan to reflect these updates, ensuring that your estate remains optimized.

Lifecycle Financial Planning for Every Stage of Life

Lifecycle financial planning focuses on managing your finances through the various phases of your life. From starting your career to raising a family and eventually retiring, each stage presents unique challenges and opportunities. Generative AI provides a dynamic approach to navigating these transitions, helping you make informed decisions and achieve financial stability.

At the beginning of your career, financial planning often revolves around building a strong foundation. Generative AI assists in creating budgets, establishing savings goals, and managing student loans or other debts. It analyzes your income, expenses, and goals to craft a personalized plan that prioritizes financial growth. For instance, it might suggest strategies for saving a portion of your salary while also paying down high-interest debt.

As you advance in your career, your financial priorities may shift toward wealth accumulation and long-term planning. Generative AI can help you identify investment opportunities that align with your risk tolerance and financial objectives. Whether it's recommending contributions to a retirement account or exploring options in real estate, AI ensures that your money works efficiently for you.

For individuals starting a family, financial planning becomes more complex. Expenses related to childcare, education, and healthcare require careful management. Generative AI simplifies this process by forecasting future costs and suggesting practical strategies to meet them. For instance, it can help you set up an education savings plan for your children or recommend insurance policies that provide comprehensive coverage at an affordable rate.

As you approach retirement, the focus of lifecycle financial planning shifts to preserving your wealth and ensuring a steady income. Generative AI provides valuable insights into how to structure your savings and investments for long-term sustainability. It can simulate different scenarios to determine the optimal withdrawal rate from your retirement accounts, balancing the need for income with the goal of preserving your principal.

In addition to financial management, AI can also address non-monetary aspects of retirement planning, such as lifestyle considerations. For example, relocating to an area with a lower cost of living or identifying hobbies and activities that fit within your budget. This holistic approach ensures that retirement is not only financially secure but also personally fulfilling.

One of the most significant benefits of Generative AI in lifecycle financial planning is its ability to anticipate challenges and provide proactive solutions. For instance, it can identify potential gaps in your financial plan, such as insufficient insurance coverage or unaccounted healthcare costs. By addressing these issues early, AI helps you avoid financial setbacks and maintain stability.

Integrating Estate and Lifecycle Planning

Estate planning and lifecycle financial planning may seem like distinct areas of financial management, but they share a vital connection that Generative AI effectively bridges by treating these elements as interwoven rather than separate. Generative AI crafts strategies that not only address your immediate financial concerns but also align with your broader, long-term aspirations.

This integration ensures that as your circumstances evolve—be it a career change, the birth of a child, or the acquisition of new assets—your financial strategy adapts seamlessly. For example, when you invest in property or inherit wealth, AI can automatically reassess your estate plan, ensuring that these assets are allocated wisely and protected. Similarly, as your lifecycle needs shift, such as preparing for retirement or funding a child's education, the AI recalibrates your approach to ensure these priorities don't conflict with your overarching financial goals.

A critical feature of Generative AI in this context is its holistic outlook. It evaluates your entire financial ecosystem, recognizing how each decision impacts another. For instance, allocating resources toward a child's college fund might appear to strain your short-term budget, but AI can identify underutilized assets or suggest optimized savings methods that meet this goal without jeopardizing your retirement plan. This comprehensive analysis fosters harmony across all financial dimensions, giving you peace of mind that every decision supports your long-term stability.

Generative AI's adaptability is another cornerstone of this integration. Life is unpredictable, and circumstances can change rapidly, whether due to economic shifts, personal milestones, or new legislation. AI tools not only keep pace with these changes but proactively suggest adjustments. For instance, if tax laws evolve, AI can identify opportunities to restructure your financial plan, ensuring compliance while maximizing benefits. This level of responsiveness reduces the risk of outdated or inefficient strategies.

Additionally, Generative AI simplifies the often-daunting coordination between estate and lifecycle planning. Traditional approaches may involve separate advisors or lengthy consultations to align these areas, but AI streamlines this process. It acts as a central hub, ensuring that updates to one aspect, such as a new investment, are reflected across your entire financial strategy. For example, if you decide to establish a trust for your children, the AI automatically adjusts your lifecycle plan to account for the funds allocated, preserving the balance between your present and future needs.

The seamless integration enabled by AI also minimizes errors and oversights. When different parts of a financial plan are managed separately, there's a higher chance of inconsistency, such as forgetting to update a beneficiary after a life event. Generative AI eliminates this risk by maintaining a unified view of your financial picture. For instance, if you marry or welcome a new child into the family, the AI ensures that these changes are reflected in your estate plan, retirement strategy, and educational savings simultaneously.

Moreover, this interconnected approach fosters better decision-making by providing a clear understanding of trade-offs. For example, if you're considering whether to downsize your home during retirement, Generative AI evaluates not only the immediate financial benefits but also the long-term implications for your estate and lifecycle plans. This insight empowers you to make choices that align with your broader objectives, whether it's preserving wealth for future generations or enhancing your quality of life.

Generative AI's ability to analyze vast amounts of data and generate personalized recommendations makes it a valuable ally in estate and lifecycle planning. Its predictive capabilities allow it to anticipate challenges before they arise, such as identifying gaps in insurance coverage or forecasting potential healthcare costs. By addressing these issues proactively, AI helps safeguard your financial stability and ensures that your plans remain resilient against unforeseen events.

The integration of estate and lifecycle planning through Generative AI enhances transparency and control. It provides clear, actionable insights into how your financial resources are being utilized and ensures that every dollar is working toward your defined goals. This transparency builds confidence, allowing you to focus on what matters most—enjoying life while securing your financial legacy.

Generative AI transforms estate and lifecycle financial planning into a cohesive, adaptive process. By recognizing their interconnected nature and continuously refining strategies to reflect your evolving circumstances, it create a financial blueprint that is both robust and flexible. This innovative approach not only simplifies complex decisions but also ensures that your financial journey is aligned with your personal and familial aspirations at every step.

Real-Life Applications and Success Stories

Generative AI has revolutionized how individuals handle estate and lifecycle financial planning, turning intricate processes into streamlined, tailored strategies. Its practical benefits can be observed in various scenarios, showcasing its ability to adapt to unique challenges and create optimal solutions.

Take the case of a young professional who recently inherited a significant sum of money. Managing newfound wealth can be daunting, but with the help of Generative AI, this individual developed a comprehensive financial roadmap. The AI system analyzed their current financial state, future aspirations, and potential risks, crafting a plan that balanced short-term liquidity with long-term investments. Beyond allocating funds into diverse assets, the system also recommended establishing a trust. This trust not only safeguarded the inheritance but ensured that it would benefit future generations in alignment with the individual's legacy goals. By offering projections on how the investments would grow over decades, the AI empowered them to make informed decisions, transforming uncertainty into confidence.

Another compelling example involves a retiree navigating changes in their family structure. After a significant life event, such as the birth of a grandchild or the loss of a spouse, many people face the challenge of updating their estate plans. For this retiree, Generative AI analyzed their revised financial situation alongside familial dynamics. The AI system identified ways to restructure their assets, suggesting fair and equitable distribution strategies that minimized tax burdens. For instance, the system proposed using tax-efficient vehicles like irrevocable trusts or charitable contributions, aligning with the retiree's values while preserving wealth for heirs. By doing so, the retiree's legacy remained intact, and their wishes were met with minimal stress and administrative burden.

Consider also the scenario of a middle-aged couple preparing for the future education costs of their children. Traditional approaches often require families to estimate costs based on general assumptions, but Generative AI offers far greater precision. By analyzing trends in tuition inflation, available scholarship opportunities, and the couple's income flow, the AI system devised a savings plan tailored to their specific needs. It proposed contributions to tax-advantaged educational savings accounts and recommended supplemental investments that could grow alongside their child's academic journey. The couple could monitor progress and receive periodic updates, ensuring they stayed on track without sacrificing other financial goals like retirement.

Generative AI's versatility is evident in cases of business owners planning their estates. One such entrepreneur, facing complexities from owning multiple businesses, used AI to map out an effective succession plan. The system accounted for the unique nature of each business, predicting future profitability and identifying suitable heirs or successors. Furthermore, the

AI highlighted areas where tax efficiency could be improved, ensuring a smooth transition without undue financial strain on the inheritors. This not only secured the entrepreneur's legacy but also maintained the stability of the businesses during the transition period.

Families dealing with blended structures—such as those with children from previous marriages—have also benefited significantly from Generative AI. One couple faced the sensitive challenge of distributing assets equitably among all family members while avoiding potential conflicts. Generative AI analyzed the family's financial picture and proposed solutions like establishing separate trusts for each child, ensuring transparency, and fairness. The couple was able to preserve family harmony while adhering to their personal values, all with minimal manual effort.

Generative AI doesn't only cater to individuals or families with large estates. Even those with modest means have found its tools invaluable in creating plans that reflect their goals. For example, a single parent balancing limited income with savings ambitions used AI to prioritize essential expenses while setting aside incremental amounts for both retirement and their child's future. By continuously adjusting the plan based on income variations, the AI ensured that no opportunity to save was overlooked.

These success stories collectively demonstrate the profound impact of Generative AI in estate and lifecycle planning. By addressing unique needs, offering actionable insights, and adapting to life's unpredictable changes, this technology empowers individuals to take control of their financial futures with clarity and confidence. From managing inheritances to safeguarding legacies, Generative AI proves its value in simplifying the complexities of wealth management for all.

EDUCATION EXPENSE AND FAMILY PLANNING WITH GENERATIVE AI

Education and family planning are two of the most significant financial commitments individuals face. Whether it's preparing for a child's education, managing ongoing family expenses, or planning for the future, these challenges often require strategic decision-making. Generative AI provides an innovative solution by offering insights, strategies, and personalized advice tailored to an individual's financial situation. This section explores how Generative AI simplifies the complexities of education and family planning, empowering families to make informed decisions.

The Rising Cost of Education

Education is often one of the most significant financial commitments for families, with costs steadily increasing over time. Beyond tuition, there are hidden expenses such as textbooks, digital resources, extracurricular fees, and accommodation, all of which can place a heavy burden on a family's finances. Generative AI offers a transformative way to navigate this challenge by acting as a predictive and planning tool. It uses vast datasets to analyze historical trends, inflation rates, and geographic variations to give a clear picture of future education costs.

For instance, a family considering private schooling for their child can utilize Generative AI to determine the likely expenses over the next decade. It doesn't just calculate tuition; it accounts for additional costs like uniforms and after-school programs, ensuring that parents have a comprehensive understanding of their financial requirements. This foresight allows families to allocate resources efficiently, balancing education savings with other long-term goals like retirement or homeownership.

Generative AI is particularly effective in tailoring predictions to specific circumstances. For example, it can identify differences in education costs based on location, type of institution, or field of study. If a child is interested in pursuing a career in technology, the AI can estimate the tuition for relevant degrees, along with expected costs for specialized equipment or certifications. Such precise insights empower families to make informed decisions about savings strategies and funding options.

Additionally, Generative AI doesn't only provide static predictions. It evolves as new data emerges, allowing families to adjust their plans dynamically. For example, if tuition fees suddenly spike due to unexpected economic factors, the AI recalibrates its recommendations, suggesting ways to make up the shortfall or explore alternative financial solutions. This adaptability ensures that families remain prepared, even in the face of uncertainty.

By simplifying the complexities of financial forecasting, Generative AI alleviates much of the anxiety associated with rising education costs. It offers clarity and confidence, enabling families to take proactive steps toward ensuring their children's access to quality education without compromising their broader financial stability.

Personalized Education Savings Plans

Every family has unique financial circumstances, and a one-size-fits-all approach rarely works when planning for education. Generative AI excels at creating personalized savings plans that adapt to a family's income, expenses, and future aspirations. These plans go beyond generic advice by factoring in specific goals, such as the desire to fund private school education or support a child's international studies.

AI tools can also suggest efficient savings vehicles, like tax-advantaged education accounts, to maximize returns. For instance, in the United States, tools powered by Generative AI might recommend 529 plans, which offer tax benefits for education savings. By analyzing the family's financial history, the AI can advise on how much to contribute each month, making the process manageable and stress-free.

Managing Uncertainties

One of the biggest challenges in education planning is accounting for uncertainties. Changes in income, unexpected expenses, or fluctuations in tuition costs can disrupt even the most well-laid plans. Generative AI mitigates these risks by continuously analyzing financial data and suggesting adjustments in real time. If a family's income unexpectedly increases, the AI might recommend reallocating some of the extra funds toward education savings. Conversely, if expenses rise, it could suggest temporary reductions in contributions without compromising the long-term goal.

In addition to financial adjustments, Generative AI provides insights into alternative funding options. These include scholarships, grants, or work-study programs that ease the financial burden. By identifying opportunities suited to the student's profile, AI helps families make informed decisions and maximize their resources.

Optimizing Education Loans

For families who may need to rely on loans, Generative AI simplifies the process of selecting and managing the best options. It evaluates various loan programs, considering factors like interest rates, repayment terms, and the family's financial health. The AI then recommends loans that minimize long-term costs while ensuring repayment remains manageable.

Once a loan is in place, Generative AI can assist in creating a repayment strategy. By analyzing the borrower's income and expenses, it suggests optimal payment schedules that reduce interest over time. This proactive approach ensures that families stay on top of their financial commitments while working toward other goals.

Holistic Family Financial Planning

Family planning extends beyond education and encompasses the broader financial needs of raising children and managing household expenses. Generative AI offers holistic solutions by considering all aspects of a family's financial life, from daily budgeting to long-term investments.

One key area where AI excels is in helping families balance competing priorities. For instance, a family may need to save for education while also building an emergency fund or paying off a mortgage. Generative AI creates comprehensive plans that allocate resources effectively, ensuring each goal receives adequate attention without overwhelming the budget.

Another advantage of Generative AI is its ability to predict and plan for life events that impact family finances. These could include the birth of a child, changes in employment, or unexpected medical expenses. By anticipating these events, AI enables families to stay prepared and maintain financial stability.

Reducing Stress with Automated Insights

One of the most significant benefits of using Generative AI for education and family planning is the reduction of stress. Financial planning can be overwhelming, particularly when it involves large expenses and long-term commitments. Generative AI simplifies the process by automating routine tasks and providing clear, actionable insights.

For example, instead of manually tracking expenses and adjusting budgets, families can rely on AI tools to do the heavy lifting. The AI categorizes expenses, identifies areas for savings, and updates plans based on real-time data. This not only saves time but also ensures that decisions are based on accurate and up-to-date information.

Building Financial Security for Future Generations

Generative AI extends its impact beyond the immediate financial needs of a family, fostering a foundation of long-term security that benefits future generations. By developing personalized investment strategies, it empowers families to grow and protect wealth in a way that ensures financial stability for their children and descendants. This forward-thinking approach to wealth management is a game-changer, especially in a rapidly changing economic landscape.

One of the primary advantages of Generative AI in building generational wealth is its ability to identify and recommend investment opportunities that align with both current resources and long-term objectives. For example, a family aiming to secure educational funds for their grandchildren may rely on AI to analyze potential investment vehicles like mutual funds, real estate, or sustainable energy projects. The AI evaluates factors such as market trends, historical performance, and future growth potential, tailoring strategies to the family's specific needs and risk appetite.

In addition to identifying investments, Generative AI plays an active role in managing and optimizing portfolios. By continuously monitoring economic conditions, it can detect shifts in market dynamics and suggest timely adjustments. This proactive approach minimizes risks while maximizing returns, ensuring that the family's financial plans remain resilient in the face of economic uncertainties. For instance, if a market downturn threatens the value of a family's assets, the AI might recommend diversifying into less volatile sectors or reallocating funds to safer instruments like government bonds.

Generative AI also facilitates intergenerational financial education, a critical element of building lasting wealth. By integrating AI tools into everyday financial management, families can encourage younger members to develop skills in budgeting, saving, and investing. These tools not only provide insights but also offer interactive features that make financial learning engaging and accessible for children and teenagers. For example, AI-driven apps might simulate investment scenarios, helping young users understand the principles of risk and return without real-world consequences.

Moreover, Generative AI contributes to estate planning, a cornerstone of generational wealth transfer. It simplifies complex processes like drafting wills, establishing trusts, and minimizing tax liabilities, ensuring that assets are distributed according to the family's wishes. By leveraging AI insights, families can identify the most efficient methods for transferring wealth while preserving its value. This might involve setting up trust funds that grow over time or creating charitable foundations that reflect the family's values, ensuring a legacy that extends beyond financial success.

The ability of Generative AI to account for multiple variables and future scenarios makes it uniquely suited to long-term planning. For example, it can analyze the impact of inflation on assets, predict shifts in tax policies, and even model the financial implications of major life events like weddings or business ventures. These insights allow families to plan with a level of precision and foresight that was previously unattainable.

Generative AI also fosters resilience by identifying and mitigating potential financial risks that could jeopardize generational wealth. Whether it's an unexpected economic downturn, regulatory changes, or shifts in market behavior, the AI provides actionable recommendations to safeguard assets. This ensures that families are not only able to grow their wealth but also protect it against unforeseen challenges.

Beyond financial stability, Generative AI helps families align their wealth-building strategies with their values. For instance, families who prioritize sustainability can use AI to identify investments in green technologies or ethical businesses. This alignment of financial goals with personal principles creates a sense of purpose and pride, reinforcing the importance of responsible wealth management.

Ultimately, Generative AI transforms the concept of wealth-building into a holistic, dynamic process that extends across generations. By combining advanced analytics with personalized recommendations, it empowers families to create and sustain financial legacies that adapt to changing circumstances and reflect their aspirations. In doing so, it not only secures the financial future of descendants but also instills a culture of informed decision-making and long-term thinking that benefits generations to come.

Real-World Success Stories

The transformative potential of Generative AI is best illustrated through real-world examples. Consider a family of four with two young children. Using an AI-driven financial planning tool, they identified the future cost of their children's college education and created a personalized savings plan. Over the years, the AI continuously updated its plan based on changes in income and expenses, ensuring it stayed on track. When the time came for their children to attend college, the family had enough saved to cover tuition without taking on significant debt. In another example, a single parent used Generative AI to manage both education savings and daily expenses. The AI tool provided actionable insights on reducing unnecessary spending and reallocating those funds toward a 529 savings plan. Over time, this strategy enabled the parent to secure a stable financial future for their child while maintaining a comfortable lifestyle.

CHAPTER 8

ETHICAL CONSIDERATIONS

INTRODUCTION: ETHICS AS THE FOUNDATION FOR GENERATIVE AI IN FINANCE

Generative AI is transforming how the financial world operates. From automating routine tasks to making predictions based on vast datasets, it offers opportunities to enhance efficiency and precision. Its ability to personalize financial recommendations has opened doors for tailored user experiences, ensuring more people can access financial solutions suited to their needs. However, these advancements come with significant responsibilities. The ethical dimensions of this technology must be carefully considered and addressed to prevent harm, ensure fairness, and maintain public trust.

The deployment of Generative AI in finance demands thoughtful governance, as it directly influences decisions that affect individuals and businesses alike. Key areas of concern include safeguarding sensitive financial information, ensuring that algorithms function without bias, and adhering to a rapidly evolving regulatory landscape. Addressing these issues is not optional; it is fundamental to building a future where Generative AI operates responsibly.

This chapter highlights the ethical challenges posed by Generative AI while offering strategies to mitigate them. By emphasizing data privacy, fairness, and compliance with regulations, organizations can strike a balance between innovation and accountability. These principles will form the cornerstone for the safe and sustainable integration of Generative AI into the financial sector.

The Importance of Data Privacy in AI-Driven Finance

Why Data Privacy Matters

Data privacy is a foundational principle in the application of Generative AI within the financial sector. The effectiveness of this technology depends on its ability to process vast amounts of information, including highly sensitive data such as bank transactions, credit histories, and personal income details. This reliance makes protecting data an essential requirement, as the misuse or exposure of such information can result in widespread harm. For individuals, breaches can mean identity theft, compromised accounts, and unauthorized financial transactions. For organizations, it can trigger legal disputes, hefty penalties, and the loss of customer trust.

When users share their financial information with AI-powered platforms, they do so under the assumption that their data will be handled with care. Failing to meet these expectations can damage the organization's credibility and discourage users from embracing innovative technologies. Beyond the immediate financial implications of a breach, there is also the risk of lasting reputational harm. Once trust is broken, rebuilding it becomes a long and arduous process.

Data privacy is more than just compliance with regulations; it is also an ethical obligation. Organizations must ensure that their systems respect the rights and dignity of individuals. This involves designing AI platforms that not only prioritize security but also reflect transparency in their operations. People have the right to know how their data is being used, why it is being collected, and what measures are in place to protect it.

Moreover, the interconnected nature of financial systems means that a single data breach can have cascading effects. A compromised dataset could expose related accounts, impact business partners, or even disrupt larger financial networks. This amplifies the importance of implementing robust privacy measures that extend beyond individual systems to safeguard the ecosystem as a whole.

In a world increasingly reliant on digital solutions, ensuring data privacy is not merely a technological challenge; it is a societal expectation. Organizations that take proactive steps to protect sensitive information and build secure systems demonstrate their commitment to ethical responsibility. By making privacy a cornerstone of their operations, these organizations not only comply with laws but also establish themselves as trustworthy stewards of user information in a rapidly evolving digital age.

How Generative AI Uses Data

Generative AI processes data to identify patterns, make predictions, and offer solutions. For example, in personalized financial planning, the AI might analyze spending habits to suggest savings strategies. In investment management, it could predict market trends based on historical data. While this is beneficial, it also raises questions about how securely the data is stored, who has access to it, and whether users are fully informed about how their information is being utilized.

Building Trust Through Transparent Practices

Establishing trust is a cornerstone of using Generative AI responsibly, especially in finance, where sensitive personal data is involved. Transparency ensures users understand how their data is handled and fosters confidence in the systems they rely on. Organizations should prioritize clear and concise communication about data collection, processing, and usage. This involves breaking down technical details into accessible language, ensuring that users can make informed choices without feeling overwhelmed by complex jargon.

Financial institutions can implement practical measures to enhance transparency. For example, creating interactive tutorials or FAQs on data policies can help users understand how their information is stored and protected. Similarly, including examples of how data is used, such as tailoring savings plans or detecting fraudulent activities, makes the benefits of Generative AI tangible and relatable.

Another key aspect of transparency is granting users control over their data. This includes giving individuals the ability to decide how much information they want to share. Options like opting out of certain types of data collection, restricting the duration for which data is stored, or enabling data portability allow users to retain ownership of their information. These features empower users to take an active role in safeguarding their privacy.

Transparency also extends to addressing potential risks. Organizations should proactively disclose any vulnerabilities or limitations in their systems, as this honesty builds credibility. For instance, financial apps using Generative AI could notify users about the possibility of algorithmic errors or biases and explain how such issues are being mitigated. This openness not only increases trust but also encourages users to provide feedback, which can help improve the technology.

Additionally, organizations should adopt mechanisms for regular user engagement. This could include sending updates about policy changes or new security features, ensuring users feel informed and valued. By fostering open communication channels, companies demonstrate their commitment to ethical practices and user empowerment.

Transparency is not just about meeting regulatory requirements—it's a long-term strategy for building loyalty. Users who feel confident that their data is handled ethically and securely are more likely to adopt and recommend AI-powered financial tools. Through clear policies, user control, and proactive communication, organizations can create a foundation of trust that benefits both the user and the broader adoption of Generative AI.

Securing Data Against Breaches

Data breaches pose one of the most significant risks in using Generative AI in finance, as they can lead to compromised personal and financial information. Financial institutions must remain proactive by implementing advanced security protocols to stay ahead of increasingly sophisticated cyber threats. Strong encryption methods ensure that data remains unintelligible to unauthorized individuals, even if intercepted. Additionally, multi-factor authentication adds a vital layer of security by requiring multiple forms of verification before granting access to sensitive systems.

Beyond securing access points, institutions must conduct regular security audits to identify vulnerabilities and rectify them before they can be exploited. These assessments help organizations remain adaptive to new threats, as cybercriminals constantly evolve their tactics. Furthermore, penetration testing can simulate potential attacks, providing valuable insights into how systems might fail under pressure and how they can be strengthened.

Data anonymization plays a key role in reducing risks when using large datasets. By stripping away identifiable details, organizations can leverage valuable insights without exposing personal information. However, anonymization is not a perfect solution. Advanced techniques, such as combining anonymized data with external datasets, can re-identify individuals, making it critical for organizations to go beyond standard anonymization practices. This includes frequent evaluations of anonymization methods to ensure they meet the highest security standards.

Institutions must also invest in secure data storage practices, such as using decentralized storage solutions or encrypted cloud systems. Decentralized storage spreads data across multiple locations, minimizing the risk of a single point of failure. Additionally, establishing clear protocols for data access ensures that only authorized personnel with a legitimate need can interact with sensitive information, thereby reducing the risk of internal breaches.

Education and training are equally important in securing data. Employees need to be aware of the latest cybersecurity threats and how to respond to them effectively. A well-informed workforce can act as the first line of defense, detecting and mitigating potential breaches before they escalate. By combining technological advancements with human vigilance, financial institutions can better protect data from unauthorized access and malicious attacks.

Institutions must foster a culture of accountability and transparency when it comes to data protection. Communicating openly with users about the measures in place to safeguard their information builds trust and demonstrates a commitment to ethical practices. A secure environment ensures not only compliance with regulations but also the long-term success and reputation of any financial organization relying on Generative AI.

THE IMPORTANCE OF DATA PRIVACY IN AI-DRIVEN FINANCE

In today's world, where data flows freely across digital networks, privacy has become a cornerstone of ethical financial practices. As Generative AI increasingly finds applications in finance, it relies on vast amounts of sensitive data to operate effectively. This reliance brings tremendous potential but also significant risks if data privacy is not managed with care. Protecting individuals' financial information is not just a technical requirement—it is a moral and legal responsibility that affects trust, security, and the integrity of the financial system.

Why Data Privacy Matters in Finance

Financial data is among the most personal and sensitive types of information. It includes details about income, spending habits, investments, debts, and even tax records. This data paints a clear picture of someone's life, making it a valuable resource for organizations but a significant risk if it falls into the wrong hands. For Generative AI to deliver meaningful insights and solutions, it must analyze this type of data. However, this process must be handled with extreme caution.

When privacy breaches occur, the consequences can be severe. Unauthorized access to financial data can lead to identity theft, fraud, or other malicious activities. For example, if an AI system is compromised, attackers could misuse the sensitive information it processes, causing financial and emotional distress to individuals and eroding trust in the technology.

Generative AI and the Data Dependency

Generative AI excels by identifying patterns and generating insights from large datasets. In finance, this means using transaction histories, market trends, credit scores, and customer profiles to predict outcomes or optimize strategies. While this capability makes Generative AI a powerful tool, it also places a heavy emphasis on data collection and storage. The more data an AI system accesses, the better it can perform, but this increased access also heightens the risks of exposure.

For example, when an AI model learns from spending data to predict future expenses or create budgets, it must handle vast amounts of financial records. If these records are not adequately protected, they could be exposed through breaches or mismanagement. This delicate balance between leveraging data and protecting it is at the heart of the privacy conversation in AI-driven finance.

The Role of Anonymization in Protecting Privacy

One way to ensure data privacy while still allowing AI to perform effectively is through anonymization. Anonymization involves removing personally identifiable information (PII) from datasets so that individuals cannot be traced back to the raw data. For instance, names, account numbers, and addresses can be replaced with codes or completely removed.

While anonymization helps reduce the risk of exposing personal details, it is not foolproof. In some cases, sophisticated attackers can re-identify individuals by cross-referencing anonymized data with other available information. This possibility underscores the need for continuous innovation in privacy-preserving techniques to stay ahead of potential threats.

Consent and Transparency as Foundations of Trust

Building trust in Generative AI systems starts with transparency. Users must be aware of how their data is collected, stored, and used. When financial institutions adopt AI technologies, they must ensure that their customers are fully informed about how their information is used. This involves clear and accessible privacy policies that explain data practices in simple terms.

Consent plays a crucial role here. Customers should have control over their data and the ability to opt out of practices with which they are uncomfortable. For example, a bank using AI for budgeting should allow customers to opt in or out of sharing their transaction history with the system. This approach not only respects individual privacy but also fosters confidence in the technology.

Data Privacy Regulations in Finance

To address the risks associated with data privacy, governments and organizations have implemented various regulations to protect sensitive information. Laws such as the General Data Protection Regulation (GDPR) in Europe and the California Consumer Privacy Act (CCPA) in the United States establish strict guidelines for the collection, use, and sharing of data. These regulations aim to ensure that organizations handle data responsibly and provide individuals with more control over their information.

For financial institutions using Generative AI, compliance with these laws is essential. They must establish processes to secure data, limit its use to specified purposes, and notify individuals in the event of a breach. Non-compliance can result in hefty fines and damage to the organization's reputation. Furthermore, these regulations encourage companies to adopt privacy-first approaches in their AI systems.

Balancing Innovation with Privacy

The drive for innovation often requires access to vast amounts of data, but this should never come at the expense of privacy. Organizations must strike a balance between advancing AI capabilities and safeguarding individuals' information. Privacy does not have to be an obstacle to innovation; rather, it can be an enabler by building trust and ensuring the ethical use of AI technologies.

For example, some companies are exploring privacy-preserving

AI models that operate on encrypted data. This means the AI can perform its tasks without ever "seeing" the raw data itself. Techniques like federated learning, where data is processed locally on users' devices instead of being centralized, are also gaining traction. These approaches demonstrate that it is possible to innovate while respecting privacy.

Protecting Against Breaches and Misuse

Even with robust systems in place, data breaches can still occur. Cybercriminals are constantly developing new methods to exploit vulnerabilities in financial systems, making it imperative for organizations to remain vigilant. Regular security audits, strong encryption practices, and secure storage protocols are essential components of a privacy-first strategy.

Additionally, organizations must consider the ethical implications of their data usage. For example, using Generative AI to predict customer behavior for targeted marketing campaigns can be beneficial, but it must be done without manipulating or exploiting customers. Ethical guidelines and internal policies should govern the use of AI to prevent misuse.

The Role of Consumers in Data Privacy

While organizations bear the primary responsibility for protecting data, consumers also play a role in safeguarding their information. Educating individuals about best practices, such as creating strong passwords, avoiding suspicious links, and monitoring financial accounts, can help reduce the risks of breaches. Additionally, consumers should be encouraged to ask questions and demand transparency from companies that handle their personal data.

For instance, a customer using a Generative AI-powered budgeting app should be aware of where their data is stored, who has access to it, and how it is being utilized. By taking an active role in their privacy, consumers can complement organizational efforts to create a secure financial ecosystem.

Privacy as a Competitive Advantage

In a market where trust is paramount, prioritizing privacy can be a competitive advantage for financial institutions. Companies that demonstrate a commitment to data protection are more likely to attract and retain customers. For example, a bank that offers clear privacy controls, detailed transparency reports, and robust security measures will likely gain an edge over competitors that do not prioritize these aspects.

This focus on privacy can also extend to brand loyalty. Customers are more likely to stay with institutions they trust, and strong privacy practices can be a cornerstone of that trust. By embedding privacy into the core of their operations, organizations can differentiate themselves and foster long-term relationships with their clients.

The Future of Data Privacy in AI-Driven Finance

As Generative AI continues to evolve, so too will the challenges and opportunities related to data privacy. Emerging technologies, such as quantum computing, are poised to transform the landscape of encryption and data security. At the same time, advancements in privacy-preserving AI methods will enable even greater protections for individuals.

The future of finance will likely involve a deeper integration of AI, making it even more critical to prioritize privacy. Organizations must remain proactive, anticipating new risks and adapting their strategies to address them. Collaboration between industry leaders, regulators, and technologists will be key to ensuring that data privacy remains a central focus in the development of AI-driven financial solutions.

ADDRESSING BIAS AND ENSURING FAIRNESS IN ALGORITHMS

Generative AI is revolutionizing the way decisions are made in finance, from credit approvals to investment strategies. However, this transformation also raises critical concerns about bias and fairness in algorithms. Bias in AI systems can have profound consequences, particularly when they are used to make financial decisions affecting people's lives. Ensuring fairness in these systems is not only an ethical responsibility but also a practical necessity for maintaining trust and efficiency in financial institutions.

Understanding Bias in Generative AI

Bias in AI algorithms stems from the data on which they are trained. Generative AI models learn patterns from historical datasets, which often reflect societal inequities or discriminatory practices. When these patterns are embedded in AI systems, the models may unintentionally perpetuate or even amplify these biases. For example, if historical lending data shows a pattern of discrimination against certain demographics, a Generative AI model trained on that data could replicate similar unfair practices in credit scoring.

Bias is not always a result of malicious intent. It often arises because data is incomplete, unbalanced, or lacks representation of diverse groups. In finance, this can lead to significant disparities, such as some groups being unfairly excluded from accessing loans, mortgages, or investment opportunities.

The Impact of Biased Algorithms in Finance

Biased algorithms in finance can create ripple effects that exacerbate inequality. For instance, if a loan approval system consistently denies applications from individuals in certain neighborhoods, it could reinforce existing economic disparities. Similarly, investment models that overlook opportunities in underrepresented markets could stifle economic growth in those areas.

Fairness in financial algorithms is essential not only for ethical reasons but also for the stability and sustainability of the financial ecosystem. When people perceive AI systems as unfair, it undermines trust in financial institutions, leading to regulatory scrutiny and reputational damage.

How Bias Enters Generative AI Systems

Several factors contribute to bias in Generative AI systems:

- Historical Data: AI models trained on historical data inherit the biases present in those records. For example, if past credit approvals favored specific demographics, the model might replicate that pattern.
- Data Imbalance: When datasets are dominated by information from certain groups while excluding others, the AI system becomes skewed toward the overrepresented group.
- Algorithm Design: Sometimes, bias originates from the design of the algorithm itself. Developers might unintentionally introduce parameters that favor certain outcomes.
- Unintentional Correlation: AI can mistakenly use irrelevant attributes as proxies for decision-making. For example, it might correlate someone's zip code with their creditworthiness, even if the two are unrelated.

Understanding these sources of bias is the first step toward addressing the issue and ensuring fairness in AI systems.

Steps to Address Bias in Generative AI

Ensuring fairness in Generative AI requires a multifaceted approach that includes data management, algorithmic improvements, and ongoing monitoring.

1. Building Diverse and Representative Datasets

The foundation of any AI model is its training data. Ensuring that this data is diverse and representative is critical to minimizing bias. In finance, this means including data from different demographic groups, geographic regions, and socioeconomic backgrounds. A more inclusive dataset allows the AI model to learn patterns that apply across a broader spectrum of users.

For example, if a credit scoring system is trained on data that includes applicants from diverse income levels and employment types, it is more likely to make fair decisions. Similarly, investment models can benefit from datasets that account for various market dynamics, ensuring that opportunities are identified in underrepresented sectors.

2. Implementing Bias Audits

Bias audits are systematic reviews of AI systems to identify and address potential disparities. These audits examine both the training data and the model's outputs to ensure that no group is unfairly disadvantaged. Financial institutions can conduct regular audits to evaluate how their AI systems perform across different demographic categories.

For example, a bank using AI for loan approvals might analyze approval rates for various ethnic groups or income brackets. If discrepancies are found, adjustments can be made to the model or the data it uses.

3. Enhancing Algorithm Transparency

Transparency is a crucial element in ensuring fairness and impartiality. Generative AI systems often function as "black boxes," meaning their decision-making processes are not easily understood. By increasing transparency, developers and users can better understand how decisions are made and identify potential sources of bias.

Explainable AI (XAI) techniques are being developed to make AI systems more interpretable. These tools break down the decision-making process into understandable components, allowing stakeholders to identify and address any biases.

4. Designing for Fairness

Developers can design algorithms with fairness in mind from the outset. This involves incorporating fairness metrics into the development process and ensuring that the model's objectives align with ethical considerations. For instance, financial algorithms can be programmed to optimize for equitable outcomes, rather than purely maximizing profitability. One approach is to use fairness constraints during the training process. These constraints ensure that the model's decisions do not disproportionately favor or disadvantage any group. For example, an investment recommendation model might be designed to distribute opportunities equally across different markets.

5. Combining Human Oversight with AI

While Generative AI can analyze data and generate insights at an unprecedented scale, it should not entirely replace human judgment. Combining AI with human oversight ensures that decisions are both accurate and ethically sound. Financial institutions can establish review processes that involve human experts validating AI-generated recommendations.

For instance, a credit approval system could flag borderline cases for manual review, allowing human evaluators to consider additional factors that the AI might have overlooked. This hybrid approach combines the efficiency of AI with the empathy and context-awareness of human decision-makers.

Measuring Fairness in Generative AI

To ensure fairness, financial institutions must establish clear metrics to evaluate their AI systems. These metrics assess whether the system's outputs are equitable across different groups.

- Disparate Impact: Measures whether an AI system's decisions disproportionately affect a specific group.
- Equal Opportunity: Ensures that all individuals, regardless

of demographic background, have an equal chance of achieving favorable outcomes.

- Demographic Parity: Evaluates whether decisions are distributed evenly across different demographic groups.

These metrics provide a framework for identifying and addressing disparities, ensuring that the AI system aligns with ethical standards.

Real-World Examples of Bias in Financial AI

Several real-world incidents highlight the importance of addressing bias in Generative AI:

- A major tech company faced backlash when its AI-driven recruitment tool was found to favor male candidates for technical roles. This bias stemmed from historical hiring data that reflected gender disparities in the industry.
- In another instance, an AI credit scoring system was criticized for approving loans at a significantly lower rate for certain ethnic groups. This issue arose because the training data failed to account for systemic inequities.

These examples underscore the need for vigilance in developing and deploying AI systems.

Ethical Benefits of Addressing Bias

Addressing bias is not just about avoiding negative consequences—it also presents significant ethical and practical benefits:

- Building Trust: Fair and transparent AI systems foster trust among users and stakeholders, enhancing the reputation of financial institutions.
- Promoting Inclusion: By addressing bias, Generative AI can empower underrepresented groups, creating more equitable financial opportunities.
- Enhancing Performance: Diverse and unbiased AI models are often more robust and perform better across a range of scenarios.

Challenges in Eliminating Bias

Despite advancements in technology and methodology, eliminating bias remains a challenging task. Some of the key challenges include:

- Implicit Bias in Data: Even with careful curation and training, data can still contain subtle biases that are difficult to detect.
- Evolving Standards: Fairness is a dynamic concept, influenced by cultural, legal, and societal changes. Ensuring that AI systems remain aligned with these evolving standards requires ongoing effort and attention.
- Resource Constraints: Conducting thorough bias audits and maintaining transparency can be resource-intensive, particularly for smaller organizations.

Generative AI holds tremendous potential to reshape the financial world, but its success depends on addressing the challenges of bias and fairness. Building systems that work equitably for all requires a shared commitment among financial institutions, developers, and regulators. This collaboration must focus on creating models that not only perform well but also align with ethical standards and societal values.

To achieve this, efforts should prioritize thoughtful innovation and rigorous testing. Developers need to design algorithms with fairness built into their foundation, while institutions must foster transparency by making AI processes easier to understand for both stakeholders and users. Regulators can play a pivotal role by establishing clear guidelines that set the standard for accountability and inclusivity.

When bias is actively managed and fairness is prioritized, Generative AI becomes a force for positive change. It can open doors to financial opportunities for underserved communities and enhance the effectiveness of decision-making for individuals and businesses. While overcoming these challenges requires persistence and adaptability, the potential to create a more inclusive and equitable financial system makes this work invaluable.

Ultimately, addressing these issues is not just about compliance or meeting standards—it's about ensuring that the transformative power of Generative AI benefits everyone.

REGULATORY COMPLIANCE AND EVOLVING LAWS IN GENERATIVE AI FOR FINANCE

The rise of Generative AI in finance brings incredible opportunities for innovation and efficiency. However, it also introduces challenges that demand careful regulation and compliance with evolving laws. Generative AI, given its ability to analyze vast amounts of data, automate complex tasks, and make predictions, requires frameworks that strike a balance between innovation, fairness, transparency, and accountability.

In the financial sector, where sensitive data and high-stakes decisions are the norm, it's crucial to address the unique risks posed by this technology. Regulatory compliance ensures that Generative AI tools and applications operate within legal boundaries while safeguarding users' rights and interests. This section explores the current state of regulations, the challenges of applying existing laws to Generative AI, and the steps businesses can take to navigate this dynamic landscape effectively.

The Need for Regulatory Oversight in Generative AI

Generative AI operates in a space that straddles technical innovation and ethical concerns. This duality makes it a powerful yet potentially risky tool in the financial sector. Without clear regulations, there's a risk of misuse, privacy breaches, discrimination, and harm to consumers. Governments, organizations, and industry leaders recognize the importance of defining boundaries to ensure that AI serves as a force for good.

Regulatory oversight aims to establish a framework that enables innovation to thrive without compromising the integrity of financial systems or the rights of individuals. This oversight addresses several critical areas, including data security, ethical decision-making, transparency in AI processes, and accountability for AI-driven outcomes.

Existing Legal Frameworks and Their Relevance to Generative AI

Although laws specifically targeting Generative AI are still developing, many existing regulations apply indirectly. These laws provide foundational principles for data handling, transparency, and accountability.

One prominent example is the General Data Protection Regulation (GDPR) in the European Union. The GDPR focuses on data privacy and security, emphasizing the need for explicit consent when collecting personal data. It also includes provisions for the "right to explanation," which mandates transparency in automated decision-making—a concept relevant to Generative AI.

In the United States, the California Consumer Privacy Act (CCPA) provides similar protections. It grants consumers rights over their data, such as the ability to know how their information is used and to opt out of its sale. These laws ensure that Generative AI applications in finance adhere to strict data privacy standards.

However, these regulations were not specifically designed for AI, let alone Generative AI. As a result, they leave gaps in areas like algorithmic accountability and fairness. For instance, while the GDPR mandates transparency, it doesn't specify how organizations should address biases in AI algorithms. These limitations highlight the need for AI-specific regulatory frameworks.

The Challenge of Applying Existing Laws to Generative AI

Generative AI presents unique challenges that existing laws may struggle to address. Traditional regulations focus on human-driven processes, whereas Generative AI involves complex algorithms making decisions that are often difficult to interpret. This complexity creates a gap between what current laws require and what AI systems can deliver.

For example, one of the biggest challenges lies in ensuring algorithmic transparency. Generative AI models, such as those based on deep learning, operate as "black boxes," meaning their decision-making processes are not easily explainable. This lack of transparency conflicts with legal requirements, such as the GDPR's "right to explanation."

Additionally, the global nature of Generative AI complicates compliance. Financial transactions often cross borders, exposing businesses to multiple legal jurisdictions. A single AI application may need to comply with the GDPR in Europe, the CCPA in California, and other regional regulations simultaneously. Harmonizing these requirements is no small feat.

Emerging Regulatory Efforts Targeting AI and Generative AI

Recognizing the limitations of existing laws, governments and international bodies are developing regulations tailored to AI technologies. These emerging frameworks aim to address the unique characteristics of Generative AI while fostering innovation.

One of the most significant efforts is the European Union's proposed AI Act. This legislation categorizes AI applications by risk level, with stricter rules applying to high-risk systems, such as those used in finance. It emphasizes transparency, accountability, and robust data protection. The AI Act also mandates risk assessments and compliance checks before deploying AI systems, ensuring that potential harms are identified and mitigated at an early stage.

In the United States, regulatory initiatives are less centralized but equally important. Agencies like the Federal Trade Commission (FTC) are issuing guidelines to ensure ethical AI practices. These efforts focus on preventing deceptive practices, ensuring fairness, and protecting consumer rights in AI applications.

Other regions, including Asia and the Middle East, are also developing AI regulations. Countries like Singapore and the United Arab Emirates are developing frameworks that strike a balance between innovation and ethical considerations. These global efforts reflect a growing consensus on the need for AI governance.

Industry Standards and Best Practices

While governments work on formal regulations, industry standards are emerging as complementary tools to guide the responsible use of Generative AI. These standards often focus on technical and operational aspects, helping organizations align their practices with ethical principles.

For instance, organizations such as the IEEE (Institute of Electrical and Electronics Engineers) and ISO (International Organization for Standardization) have developed guidelines for the ethical design and deployment of AI. These standards address issues such as bias mitigation, data security, and human oversight.

Adopting industry standards can help businesses stay ahead of regulatory requirements. By implementing best practices voluntarily, organizations demonstrate their commitment to the ethical use of AI, earning consumer trust and reducing regulatory risks.

Compliance Strategies for Businesses Using Generative AI

Navigating the regulatory landscape requires a proactive approach. Businesses must implement strategies that ensure compliance while maintaining operational efficiency and effectiveness. These strategies include:

- **Establishing AI Governance Committees:** Creating dedicated teams to oversee AI ethics, compliance, and risk management ensures that Generative AI applications align with legal and ethical standards.
- **Conducting Regular Audits:** Routine evaluations of AI models and processes help identify and address potential compliance issues. These audits should include assessments of data handling, algorithmic fairness, and transparency in decision-making.
- **Implementing Risk Assessments:** Before deploying Generative AI systems, businesses should evaluate potential risks, including bias, security vulnerabilities, and unintended consequences.
- **Collaborating with Regulators:** Engaging with regulatory bodies in the early stages of AI development fosters mutual understanding and compliance readiness. Regulatory sandboxes, where businesses can test AI applications under controlled conditions, are valuable tools in this regard.
- **Training Employees:** Educating employees about AI ethics

and compliance ensures that teams are equipped to manage regulatory challenges effectively.

The Role of Transparency in Building Trust

Transparency is a cornerstone of both regulatory compliance and the ethical use of AI. For Generative AI to gain widespread acceptance in finance, users must trust the technology. Transparency initiatives help achieve this by clarifying how AI systems operate and make decisions.

One way to enhance transparency is through explainable AI (XAI). Explainable AI techniques make it possible to understand and interpret the outputs of Generative AI models. In finance, this means providing clear justifications for decisions such as credit approvals, investment recommendations, or risk assessments.

Another important aspect of transparency is communication. Organizations must clearly explain their use of Generative AI in terms that non-technical users can understand. This includes outlining data usage policies, decision-making processes, and safeguards against misuse.

Future Challenges and Opportunities

As regulations continue to evolve, businesses face both challenges and opportunities in adopting Generative AI responsibly. On the one hand, complying with complex and varying regulations can be resource-intensive. On the other hand, robust compliance efforts can differentiate businesses in a competitive market.

One major challenge is keeping pace with the rapid development of AI technology. As Generative AI evolves, so do the risks and regulatory requirements associated with it. Businesses must remain agile, updating their practices to reflect new developments.

At the same time, emerging regulations present opportunities to build trust and credibility. By adhering to high standards, businesses can position themselves as leaders in the ethical use of AI. This not only enhances their reputation but also attracts customers who value transparency and responsibility.

CHAPTER 9

CONTENT CREATION USING GENERATIVE AI

In today's fast-paced digital world, creating clear, engaging, and professional content has become essential for effectively communicating financial strategies. Whether for businesses, financial advisors, or individuals managing their finances, the need for high-quality materials, such as reports, presentations, blogs, and other formats, is undeniable. Generative AI has transformed this landscape, enabling users to create impactful content more efficiently and with remarkable precision.

This chapter examines how Generative AI facilitates content creation in finance, simplifies complex topics, enhances decision-making through practical examples, and improves communication with cutting-edge visualization tools.

Understanding Content Creation with Generative AI

Generative AI refers to a class of artificial intelligence models designed to generate new content, whether in the form of text, images, or data visualizations. In the context of finance, these tools can process vast amounts of raw data, identify patterns, and produce coherent, accurate, and tailored written or visual content.

For example, financial advisors can use Generative AI to generate monthly performance reports that summarize their clients' investments. At the same time, companies can create detailed presentations that explain business strategies or annual growth.

These tasks, which often take hours or days to complete manually, can now be finished within minutes using AI tools.

Applications of Generative AI in Financial Content Creation

Generative AI has found numerous applications in the creation of financial content. Below are the key areas where this technology excels:

1. Generating Detailed Financial Reports

Reports are a cornerstone of financial communication, whether for corporate board meetings, investment updates, or tax summaries. Generative AI streamlines the creation of such documents by automatically analyzing data, identifying trends, and presenting insights clearly and professionally.

AI tools like ChatGPT and Jasper can help generate narratives for reports by:

- Summarizing performance metrics.
- Highlighting areas of concern or opportunities for improvement.
- Forecasting future outcomes based on historical data.
- These AI-generated reports not only save time but also reduce the likelihood of human error, ensuring greater accuracy.

2. Crafting Professional Presentations

Presentations often serve as visual aids in conveying complex financial strategies or performance reviews. Generative AI enhances presentation creation by:

- Automatically designing slides based on provided data.
- Creating data-driven visuals like graphs and charts.
- Offering suggestions for structuring the presentation in a logical, audience-friendly manner.

For instance, AI-powered tools like Beautiful.ai or Canva, equipped with AI enhancements, allow users to input raw data and receive polished presentations in minutes. This means professionals can focus more on delivery rather than spending hours on slide design.

3. Blogging and Article Writing for Finance

Blogs and articles are valuable tools for educating audiences and building trust in financial expertise. Generative AI simplifies blogging by:

- Generating topic ideas based on trending searches or industry news.
- Writing clear, concise articles tailored to different audience levels.
- Optimizing content for search engines, increasing visibility, and reach.

For example, a financial blog might discuss "How to Save for Retirement in the AI Era." Using Generative AI, the blog can include examples, actionable tips, and data-driven insights, all crafted in a tone suited to the target audience.

Simplifying Complex Financial Concepts

One of the greatest challenges in financial communication is simplifying technical jargon and complex concepts for audiences who may not have a financial background. Generative AI excels in this area by translating dense financial data into digestible content.

Breaking Down Data into Simple Narratives AI can take raw financial data, such as income statements, market trends, or investment growth projections, and summarize it in plain language. For instance, instead of presenting a table filled with numbers, an AI tool might create a summary like:

"Over the past quarter, your investments have grown by 12%, primarily driven by technology sector gains. Moving forward, we recommend diversifying into energy and healthcare to balance risk."

Creating Personalized Summaries: Generative AI can tailor content to individual preferences or knowledge levels. For instance, an AI tool might generate a highly technical report for analysts while simultaneously creating a simplified version for individual investors.

Real-World Examples of AI-Generated Financial Content

The impact of Generative AI in finance is best demonstrated through real-world applications:

CASE 1: AI-Powered Investor Reports

A mid-sized investment firm used Generative AI to create customized reports for over 500 clients. By automating the process, the firm reduced production time from three weeks to two days while maintaining high-quality insights. Clients received reports that included portfolio performance summaries, risk analyses, and tailored investment recommendations.

CASE 2: Corporate Annual Reviews

A global tech company integrated Generative AI into its financial reporting process. AI tools gathered data from multiple departments and generated a comprehensive annual review. The result was a polished, professional report that required minimal human intervention, saving the company both time and resources.

CASE 3: Blogs and Educational Content

A fintech startup leveraged Generative AI to produce blog content discussing financial literacy topics such as budgeting, saving, and ethical investing. These AI-generated articles helped the company attract a broader audience, leading to a 40% increase in website traffic within six months.

Enhancing Communication Through Visualization

Visual aids are crucial in financial content, as they help audiences understand complex data at a glance. Generative AI supports this by creating dynamic and engaging visuals:

1. Data-Driven Charts and Graphs: AI tools can automatically convert raw numbers into visually appealing charts, such as bar graphs, pie charts, and heat maps. These visuals are especially useful in reports or presentations where quick comprehension is key.
2. Scenario Modeling and Simulations: Generative AI can model various financial scenarios and present the outcomes in a visual format. For instance, a business might simulate the financial impact of expanding into a new market, with AI generating both the written explanation and the corresponding visuals.
3. Interactive Dashboards: AI-driven dashboards enable users to interact with data, exploring various metrics in real-time. For example, a financial advisor could use a dashboard to show a client how different investment strategies might perform under various market conditions.

Advantages of Using Generative AI for Content Creation

The adoption of Generative AI in financial content creation comes with numerous benefits:

- Time Efficiency: Tasks that once took days can now be completed in hours or minutes.
- Cost Savings: Automating content creation reduces the need for large teams or outsourcing, cutting overall costs.
- Consistency: AI ensures that tone, style, and formatting remain consistent across all materials, enhancing professionalism.
- Scalability: Generative AI enables users to produce large volumes of content quickly, making it ideal for growing businesses.

Challenges and Ethical Considerations

Despite its many advantages, using Generative AI for content creation also presents challenges:

1. Ensuring Data Accuracy, AI-generated content is only as good as the data it is trained on. Users must validate the information to avoid errors.
2. Avoiding Over-Reliance. While AI can automate many tasks, human oversight is necessary to ensure that the content aligns with the intended message and audience.
3. When using client data to create personalized content, businesses must prioritize data privacy and ensure compliance with regulations such as the GDPR or CCPA.

The Future of AI in Financial Content Creation

The role of Generative AI in content creation is poised to expand. Future advancements may include:

- Real-Time Content Updates: AI tools that continuously update reports or blogs as new data becomes available.
- Deeper Personalization: Generative AI models capable of understanding not just financial data but also the emotional tone or preferences of the audience.
- Immersive Experiences: The integration of AI with virtual reality (VR) and augmented reality (AR) has the potential to revolutionize the presentation of financial content.

LEVERAGING AI FOR FINANCIAL CONTENT CREATION

In an era dominated by data, the ability to communicate effectively is as crucial as the strategies themselves. Generative AI has become a transformative tool in crafting financial content, allowing professionals to produce high-quality reports, presentations, and blogs with unprecedented ease. By automating routine tasks and enhancing creative processes, Generative AI not only saves time but also elevates the quality of communication, making complex financial concepts accessible to a wider audience.

The Role of AI in Financial Storytelling

Financial data can be intimidating, often buried in spreadsheets and charts that require specialized knowledge to interpret. However, storytelling is a powerful way to make numbers meaningful, transforming them into actionable insights. Generative AI excels at this by taking raw data and creating narratives that connect with diverse audiences.

For instance, a financial analyst tasked with creating an annual performance report can utilize AI tools to automatically generate a draft, seamlessly integrating data points into a cohesive narrative. These AI-generated reports often highlight trends, pinpoint anomalies, and suggest actionable insights, freeing up analysts to focus on strategic decision-making.

Generative AI tools, such as ChatGPT or Jasper AI, are adept at producing polished and engaging content that aligns with a company's goals. They understand tone, context, and intent, enabling professionals to create materials that resonate with audiences ranging from executives to entry-level employees.

From Data to Insightful Reports

Reports are a cornerstone of financial communication, serving as a bridge between raw data and actionable strategies. Traditionally, creating comprehensive reports is a time-consuming process that requires gathering data, analyzing trends, and drafting content. With Generative AI, this process is streamlined.

AI tools analyze massive datasets within moments, identifying patterns and trends that might take a human analyst days to uncover. For example, if a company wants to review its quarterly performance, an AI model can quickly pull data from multiple sources, summarize key metrics, and draft a well-structured report. The result is not just faster reporting but also enhanced accuracy and insight.

Moreover, AI-generated reports can be customized for different audiences. A detailed version might cater to analysts, while a simplified, visually appealing version can be shared with stakeholders who prefer a high-level overview. This flexibility ensures that the same data serves diverse purposes without requiring significant additional effort.

Creating Presentations That Engage

Presentations are essential for sharing financial strategies and insights, whether in boardrooms, investor meetings, or internal reviews. However, crafting compelling presentations can be challenging, especially when dealing with complex financial data. Generative AI streamlines this process by automating much of the content creation.

Using AI, professionals can input raw financial data and receive suggestions for slides that are not only informative but also visually appealing. These tools can generate charts, graphs, and even slide narratives, ensuring that the content is clear and engaging. For example, AI can transform dense spreadsheets into visually intuitive infographics, making it easier for audiences to grasp key points.

Another benefit of AI-driven presentations is adaptability. If the data changes shortly before a meeting, AI tools can quickly update the presentation to reflect the new numbers, saving time and reducing stress. This adaptability ensures that the content remains always relevant and up-to-date, a critical factor in fast-paced industries such as finance.

Blogs That Educate and Inspire

In the digital age, blogs serve as a powerful medium for financial professionals to share knowledge, establish credibility, and connect with a broader audience. However, maintaining a consistent flow of high-quality content can be daunting. Generative AI addresses this challenge by assisting with ideation, drafting, and editing.

AI tools can identify trending topics within the financial sector, analyze audience preferences, and suggest blog ideas tailored to specific niches. For example, a wealth management firm might use AI to generate blog posts on subjects like "Smart Investing Strategies for Millennials" or "How to Navigate Market Volatility." These posts can be optimized for search engines, ensuring greater visibility and engagement.

AI also excels at creating content that is both accurate and accessible. It can take complex topics, such as tax optimization strategies or investment risk analysis, and present them in a way that resonates with non-expert readers. By doing so, AI helps professionals connect with audiences who might otherwise feel excluded from financial discussions.

Simplifying Complex Financial Concepts

One of the greatest strengths of Generative AI is its ability to make complicated ideas simple and understandable. Financial topics often involve intricate calculations, industry-specific jargon, and a level of abstraction that can be difficult for non-expert audiences to understand. AI overcomes these barriers by presenting information in a relatable, digestible format.

For example, instead of describing an investment strategy using dense technical terms, an AI-generated blog might compare it to planting a garden, explaining how diversifying investments is similar to planting different crops to ensure a bountiful harvest. These analogies make complex ideas relatable, increasing audience engagement and comprehension.

Additionally, AI can generate summaries of lengthy reports, extracting the most critical information and presenting it concisely. This feature is particularly valuable for busy professionals who need quick insights without having to delve into extensive documents. By simplifying communication, AI empowers individuals to make informed decisions with confidence.

Real-World Applications in Financial Content Creation

Generative AI's impact on financial content creation is already evident in various real-world scenarios:

- Corporate Reports: Companies use AI to generate quarterly and annual reports that integrate data, analysis, and narrative in a cohesive format. These reports not only save time but also ensure consistency across multiple iterations.
- Investor Communications: Investment firms utilize AI to craft updates for clients, summarizing portfolio performance and market trends in a clear and accessible manner.
- Educational Content: Financial educators leverage AI to create tutorials, blog posts, and videos that explain fundamental concepts to beginners, making financial literacy more accessible.

For instance, a fintech startup used AI to create a series of blog posts on cryptocurrency investing. By analyzing user behavior and preferences, the AI tailored the content to address common questions, resulting in increased readership and customer engagement.

Enhancing Visual Communication

Visuals are a vital component of financial content, as they help audiences interpret data more effectively. Generative AI tools excel at creating dynamic visuals, from simple bar charts to complex heatmaps and interactive dashboards. These visuals not only enhance understanding but also make presentations more engaging and effective.

For example, an AI tool might analyze a company's revenue data and generate a series of graphs that illustrate trends over time. These graphs can be integrated into presentations or reports, providing a clear visual representation of the data. AI also enables the creation of interactive visuals, allowing users to explore data in real-time, which is particularly valuable for strategy sessions and investor meetings.

Transforming Communication Strategies

Beyond creating individual pieces of content, Generative AI has the potential to transform entire communication strategies. By automating repetitive tasks and offering new creative possibilities, AI allows professionals to focus on strategic thinking and innovation. For example, a marketing team at a financial firm might utilize AI to create an entire campaign, encompassing blog posts, social media updates, whitepapers, and client emails. This comprehensive approach ensures consistency in messaging while reducing the workload on human teams.

Moreover, AI's ability to analyze audience data ensures that the content is tailored to resonate with specific demographics. Whether targeting millennials with advice on student loan repayment or retirees with tips on estate planning, AI-driven content is precise and effective.

The Future of AI in Financial Content Creation

As Generative AI continues to evolve, its applications in financial content creation will expand. Future advancements include real-time content adaptation, deeper integration with data analytics, and the ability to create immersive experiences utilizing technologies such as augmented reality (AR) and virtual reality (VR).

Imagine attending a virtual investor meeting where AI generates live updates on market performance, accompanied by 3D visualizations that participants can interact with. These innovations will not only enhance communication but also redefine how financial professionals engage with their audiences.

SIMPLIFYING COMPLEX FINANCIAL CONCEPTS WITH AI FOR DIVERSE AUDIENCES

In the financial world, complexity often creates barriers. Whether it's decoding technical jargon, analyzing intricate data, or making sense of market trends, the challenges can feel overwhelming. Generative AI, however, offers a powerful solution. By transforming complex financial concepts into clear, digestible insights, AI empowers diverse audiences to make informed decisions. In this section, we explore how AI achieves this and examine real-world examples where it has improved decision-making and accessibility in finance.

Breaking Down Complexity: The Role of Generative AI

Generative AI stands out for its ability to analyze and interpret vast amounts of data, distilling them into meaningful and understandable content. Traditional methods of explaining financial topics often rely on static presentations, dense language, or assumptions about the audience's prior knowledge. AI changes this by adapting content dynamically, tailoring its approach to the specific needs of the audience.

For example, imagine trying to explain the concept of compound interest to two very different groups: a high school economics class and a room full of experienced investors. While the core idea remains the same, the way it's presented must differ. Generative AI adjusts its tone, depth, and vocabulary to match the audience, ensuring the information is neither too basic nor overly complex. It achieves this by using natural language processing (NLP) to evaluate context and provide clear, relevant explanations.

Enhancing Accessibility with Visual and Written Simplicity

One of AI's strongest suits is its ability to create visuals and written content that simplifies abstract concepts. In financial contexts, visuals like graphs, charts, and infographics often speak louder than words. Generative AI can design these visuals based on user data, making them precise and easy to understand.

For instance:

- A pie chart illustrating spending habits across categories such as groceries, entertainment, and savings can help users immediately grasp their financial patterns.
- A line graph projecting future investment growth simplifies discussions about portfolio performance over time.

In written content, AI algorithms ensure clarity by avoiding technical jargon. Suppose a financial planner needs to explain diversification in an investment portfolio. In that case, AI can create content by comparing it to a concept everyone understands, such as spreading seeds in different parts of a garden to increase the likelihood of growth. Such analogies make complex topics relatable without sacrificing accuracy.

REAL-WORLD APPLICATIONS: AI IN FINANCIAL COMMUNICATION

Organizations and individuals are already using generative AI to enhance financial communication. Below are some real-world examples that demonstrate its impact on decision-making.

1. Personalized Financial Reports Financial advisors often face the challenge of presenting reports to clients with varying levels of expertise. AI solves this by tailoring these reports to individual clients. For a client with little financial background, AI-generated reports emphasize visual summaries, such as color-coded charts and simple explanations. For more

advanced clients, the same report might include detailed analyses of market trends and statistical projections.

One wealth management firm, for example, implemented an AI tool to create tailored monthly reports for its clients. The result was a 40% reduction in client queries, as the information was more understandable and aligned with their expectations.

2. Market Analysis for Small Businesses Small businesses often struggle with interpreting market trends, which can hinder their strategic planning. Generative AI helps by analyzing market data and presenting actionable insights in a simplified manner. For instance, an AI tool might identify a pattern of rising raw material costs and recommend alternative suppliers or cost-cutting strategies.

A retail company used AI to monitor customer spending behavior during seasonal sales. The AI not only identified their most profitable product categories but also suggested promotional strategies based on competitor data. This insight led to a 25% increase in sales during the next quarter.

3. Investment Simulations for Beginners. Investing can be intimidating for those new to the field. Generative AI platforms guide beginners by simulating different investment scenarios, showing potential outcomes based on market conditions. This removes the fear of the unknown and builds confidence.

A fintech app used AI to create an interactive experience for first-time investors. Users could input hypothetical amounts, select investment types, and see predicted growth over time. By presenting this information visually, the app increased user engagement and helped new investors feel more secure about their choices.

4. Government and Public Sector Use Public finance departments often deal with complex budgets and policies that need to be communicated to citizens. AI simplifies this by generating materials that explain budget allocations, tax policies, and social programs in plain language.

For example, a city council in Europe utilized AI to generate summaries of its annual budget. Instead of dense, technical documents, the summaries included infographics showing how funds were allocated to education, healthcare, and infrastructure. Public feedback improved significantly as residents felt more informed and involved.

DECISION-MAKING MADE EASIER WITH AI

One of the most powerful aspects of Generative AI is its ability to improve decision-making. Whether for individuals, businesses, or policymakers, clear and actionable information is crucial for making informed decisions. Generative AI excels in delivering this clarity by merging data analysis with human-centered communication.

1. AI-Driven Tools for Individuals. For personal finance, AI tools offer users insights that they might otherwise overlook.

For example, an AI tool that tracks spending habits can alert users when they are nearing their budget limits. Beyond simple alerts, the tool suggests adjustments, such as reallocating funds from discretionary spending to essential savings.

2. Strategic Insights for Businesses. In the corporate world, decision-making often hinges on analyzing large datasets. Generative AI provides predictive insights that enable businesses to anticipate trends and adjust their strategies accordingly. For instance, during the COVID-19 pandemic, AI tools helped companies predict shifts in consumer behavior, allowing them to adjust their offerings in real-time.
3. Policy Development for Governments Policymakers rely on clear data to develop effective policies. AI simplifies complex economic models, allowing leaders to assess the potential impact of various policy options. By presenting simulations and projections in user-friendly formats, AI ensures that decisions are both data-driven and accessible to stakeholders.

Addressing Challenges in Simplification

While Generative AI is a powerful tool, it is not without challenges. One potential issue is the risk of oversimplifying complex topics to the point where important nuances are lost. To mitigate this, AI platforms include settings that allow users to choose the level of detail they require. Additionally, combining AI-generated content with expert reviews ensures accuracy and depth.

Another challenge is ensuring that AI does not introduce bias in its analysis or communication. For example, if an AI tool relies on historical data that contains biases, it might unintentionally perpetuate them. Ongoing refinement of AI algorithms is essential to maintaining fairness and objectivity.

One of the key benefits of using AI to simplify financial concepts is the trust it builds between communicators and their audiences. When individuals or businesses feel confident in their understanding of financial matters, they are more likely to engage with tools, services, or advisors. Generative AI's ability to deliver clarity and precision fosters this trust, ensuring stronger relationships and better outcomes.

The Future of Simplified Financial Communication

As Generative AI continues to evolve, its applications in financial communication will expand. Future advancements may include real-time conversational AI tools that provide instant explanations during financial consultations, augmented reality (AR) overlays for interactive presentations, and even voice assistants that deliver insights in a conversational format.

By making financial concepts accessible to all, Generative AI ensures that knowledge is no longer a barrier to financial empowerment. As this technology becomes more integrated into daily life, it will continue to transform the way we understand

and interact with the world of finance.

Simplifying Complex Financial Concepts with AI for Diverse Audiences

In the financial world, complexity often creates barriers. Whether it's decoding technical jargon, analyzing intricate data, or making sense of market trends, the challenges can feel overwhelming. Generative AI, however, offers a powerful solution. By transforming complex financial concepts into clear, digestible insights, AI empowers diverse audiences to make informed decisions. In this section, we explore how AI achieves this and examine real-world examples where it has improved decision-making and accessibility in finance.

CONCLUSION

EMBRACING GENERATIVE AI AS A TRANSFORMATIVE TOOL

Generative AI stands as one of the most groundbreaking advancements of our time. Its ability to analyze, learn, and create new solutions has the potential to completely transform the way we approach finance, whether on a personal level or within the framework of businesses. At its core, Generative AI is not merely a tool; it is an innovation partner, helping individuals and organizations navigate the complexities of modern financial landscapes.

The Transformative Power of Generative AI

Unlike traditional tools or methods that rely solely on historical data or fixed algorithms, Generative AI adapts, evolves, and offers solutions tailored to specific needs. This flexibility makes it uniquely powerful for financial applications. Consider how difficult it can be to manually track expenses, plan for long-term goals, or predict market trends. Generative AI simplifies these tasks by not only performing them automatically but also providing insights and predictions that were previously inaccessible.

For example, a generative AI tool can analyze your spending habits, identify patterns, and suggest a tailored budgeting plan. It doesn't stop there—it can adjust that plan dynamically as your income, expenses, or goals change. This adaptability saves time, eliminates human error, and provides a level of financial insight that would otherwise require significant expertise or effort. On a broader scale, businesses can use Generative AI to forecast trends, mitigate risks, and develop strategies that align with market demands. Its ability to process vast amounts of data and generate actionable insights makes it indispensable in competitive industries. Generative AI doesn't just answer questions—it asks them, exploring possibilities that even the most seasoned professionals might overlook.

Why Generative AI Matters in Finance

Finance, by its very nature, is a field of uncertainty. Markets fluctuate, personal circumstances change, and global events can send shockwaves through economies. Navigating this uncertainty requires tools that can think ahead, adapt to change, and offer guidance based on a deep understanding of both historical data and current trends. Generative AI fulfills these needs in ways that traditional systems cannot.

One of the key strengths of Generative AI is its predictive capability. It doesn't just analyze what has already happened; it anticipates what could happen next. This foresight is invaluable for making informed decisions, whether you are deciding where to invest, planning for retirement, or managing business risks. Generative AI provides a safety net in uncertain times, giving users the confidence to act boldly without fear of unforeseen consequences.

Moreover, Generative AI democratizes access to advanced financial tools. In the past, high-level financial planning and analysis were often reserved for those who could afford expensive consultants or had specialized knowledge. Today, anyone with access to AI-powered tools can benefit from personalized advice, detailed forecasts, and innovative solutions. This accessibility levels the playing field, empowering individuals and small businesses to compete and thrive in ways once unimaginable.

Practical Benefits of Generative AI

The practical applications of Generative AI in finance are both diverse and impactful. Consider how it streamlines budgeting. Traditionally, budgeting involves manually tracking expenses, setting limits, and constantly revisiting those limits to ensure adherence. Generative AI takes on this responsibility, analyzing your financial behavior and creating a budget that aligns with your lifestyle and goals. More importantly, it can adapt in real-time, accounting for unexpected changes such as a pay raise, new expenses, or shifts in priorities.

In investments, Generative AI is an invaluable resource. It can analyze market data to identify trends, simulate various market scenarios, and recommend investment strategies that maximize returns while minimizing risk. This capability is not only useful for experienced investors but also for beginners who may lack the knowledge or confidence to navigate the complexities of the stock market.

Beyond budgeting and investing, Generative AI enhances savings strategies by automating the allocation of funds. For example, it can analyze your spending patterns and identify areas where you can save more, then automatically transfer those savings into a designated account. Over time, these small adjustments can lead to significant financial growth, all without requiring active intervention from the user.

Businesses also benefit, particularly in areas such as risk management and fraud detection. Generative AI can identify vulnerabilities in a company's financial structure, predict potential risks, and suggest mitigation strategies. In fraud detection, its ability to analyze patterns and detect anomalies makes it a powerful tool for protecting assets and maintaining customer trust.

Challenges and Ethical Considerations

While the potential of Generative AI is immense, it is important to approach its adoption thoughtfully. One of the key challenges is ensuring data privacy. Generative AI relies on vast amounts of data to function effectively, and this data often includes sensitive financial information. Safeguarding this data against breaches or misuse is critical to maintaining trust and ensuring that the technology is used responsibly.

Another concern is bias. Like any AI system, Generative AI learns from the data it is trained on. If that data contains biases—whether intentional or not—the AI can perpetuate those biases in its outputs. For example, an AI model trained on biased financial data may favor certain demographics over others, resulting in unfair outcomes. Addressing this issue requires ongoing monitoring, transparency, and a commitment to fairness in both development and application.

Regulatory compliance is another important consideration. As AI continues to evolve, so too will the laws and regulations governing its use. Staying compliant requires a proactive approach, including regular audits and updates to ensure that AI systems meet current standards.

A Vision for the Future

Despite these challenges, the future of Generative AI in finance is incredibly promising. As the technology continues to advance, its capabilities will only grow, opening up new possibilities for innovation and efficiency. Imagine a world where financial decisions are not only easier but also smarter—where individuals can achieve their goals with minimal stress, and businesses can adapt to change with agility and confidence.

Generative AI has the potential to drive this vision forward, creating a financial ecosystem that is more accessible, equitable, and resilient. By embracing this technology, we can unlock opportunities that were once out of reach, setting the stage for a future defined by innovation and prosperity.

Taking the First Step

The journey to integrating Generative AI into your financial life begins with understanding its potential and taking actionable steps to leverage its capabilities. For individuals, this may involve exploring AI-powered budgeting tools or utilizing robo-advisors to manage investments. For businesses, it could involve integrating AI into financial workflows or investing in AI literacy for employees.

No matter where you start, the key is to remain open to change and committed to growth. Generative AI is not a one-size-fits-all solution; it is a tool that adapts to your unique needs and goals. By using it strategically, you can take control of your financial future and unlock new levels of success.

Building Confidence in Generative AI

One of the most significant barriers to adopting new technologies is fear of the unknown. Generative AI, with its advanced capabilities and complex mechanisms, can initially seem intimidating. However, by taking the time to understand how it works and seeing its practical benefits, users can build the confidence needed to fully embrace it.

Trust is another important factor. Building trust in Generative AI requires transparency, both from the developers creating the tools and the individuals or organizations using them. By prioritizing clear communication and ethical practices, we can create an environment where AI is seen not as a threat but as a valuable partner in achieving financial success.

GENERATIVE AI'S REVOLUTIONARY POTENTIAL IN FINANCE

Generative AI is not just another technological advancement; it is a groundbreaking force that is reshaping how individuals and businesses approach finance. From its ability to create predictive models to its capacity for crafting personalized strategies, Generative AI offers innovative solutions to long-standing financial challenges. This conclusion highlights its transformative potential, summarizing how it can revolutionize personal and business finance while inspiring action to harness its full potential.

Finance has always been a field rooted in precision, analysis, and decision-making. Traditional financial systems have relied heavily on static data and manual processes, often requiring significant human intervention to ensure accuracy and relevance. Generative AI, however, changes the game entirely. By processing vast amounts of data, identifying patterns, and generating new insights, this technology unlocks possibilities that were once out of reach.

Consider personal finance as an example. Managing finances has always required a delicate balance of planning, monitoring, and adjusting to unforeseen changes. Traditionally, this process involved manually creating budgets, tracking expenses through spreadsheets, and relying on static financial advice. With Generative

AI, these tasks are not only automated but also enhanced with real-time adaptability. Imagine a system that tracks your spending, predicts future expenses based on trends, and adjusts your budget dynamically to accommodate changes in your income or goals. This level of precision and personalization is only possible through Generative AI, which learns and adapts to your unique financial habits.

For businesses, the impact of Generative AI is equally transformative. Companies face the challenge of navigating complex markets, optimizing operations, and staying ahead of competition. Generative AI empowers businesses by offering tools to analyze trends, predict market shifts, and develop innovative strategies tailored to their specific needs. Instead of relying solely on historical data, businesses can use AI to explore future scenarios, identifying opportunities and risks with unprecedented clarity. Whether it's optimizing cash flow, mitigating risks, or creating investment portfolios, Generative AI enables businesses to operate with agility and foresight.

One of the most revolutionary aspects of Generative AI is its ability to create entirely new financial models. Unlike traditional AI, which is limited to analyzing existing data, Generative AI can generate fresh insights by identifying opportunities that are not immediately apparent. For instance, in investment management, AI can simulate multiple market scenarios to test the resilience of portfolios under various conditions. This capability allows both novice investors and seasoned professionals to make more informed decisions, ultimately leading to better financial outcomes.

The automation that Generative AI brings is another critical factor in its transformative potential. Financial tasks that once consumed significant time and resources can now be completed in a fraction of the time. Expense tracking, for instance, is no longer a tedious process requiring manual input. Generative AI can analyze transactions, categorize them accurately, and provide comprehensive reports—all while learning and improving its accuracy over time. This efficiency is particularly valuable in a world where time is money.

Yet, the true power of Generative AI lies not just in automation but in its ability to foster innovation. It enables individuals and businesses to think beyond traditional constraints, exploring possibilities that were previously inaccessible. For example, AI can generate tailored savings plans that align with both short-term and long-term goals, adapting as life circumstances change. A young professional saving for their first home and a retiree planning for medical expenses can both benefit from solutions uniquely suited to their needs.

Risk management is another area where Generative AI shines. The financial landscape is fraught with uncertainty, from market volatility to unforeseen expenses. Generative AI excels at analyzing patterns and predicting potential risks, giving users the tools to prepare and protect their assets. For instance, it can monitor investment portfolios and provide alerts when market conditions signal potential losses, enabling timely interventions. Similarly, businesses can use AI to identify operational risks and implement strategies to mitigate them before they escalate.

Fraud detection is a particularly noteworthy application. Financial fraud is a growing concern for both individuals and organizations. Generative AI's ability to identify unusual patterns in data makes it an invaluable tool for detecting and preventing fraudulent activities. By constantly learning from new data, AI systems can stay ahead of evolving threats, providing a level of security that traditional methods cannot match.

Moreover, Generative AI contributes to more ethical and sustainable financial practices. It has the potential to address biases in traditional systems, promoting fairness and inclusivity. For example, AI can help individuals align their investments with their values by identifying ethical and sustainable options that align with their financial goals. This alignment not only enhances financial outcomes but also contributes to broader societal benefits.

Long-term financial planning is another domain where Generative AI offers unparalleled advantages. Planning for the future has always been a daunting task, often involving numerous variables and uncertainties. Generative AI simplifies this process by providing tools that account for a wide range of factors, from retirement savings to estate planning. It can project future scenarios based on current data, offering actionable insights that empower users to make proactive decisions. Whether it's determining how much to save for retirement or planning for a child's education, Generative AI provides clarity and confidence.

However, it is essential to recognize that the adoption of Generative AI in finance comes with responsibilities. Ethical considerations, such as data privacy and algorithmic fairness, must be at the forefront of its implementation. Individuals and organizations must ensure that their use of AI respects privacy and promotes transparency. By addressing these challenges, Generative AI can become a trusted ally in financial management.

The role of Generative AI in finance is not limited to solving existing problems; it is about creating new opportunities. As technology continues to evolve, the potential applications of Generative AI will expand, opening doors to innovations we have yet to imagine. The financial strategies of tomorrow will be defined by those who embrace this technology today, using it not just as a tool but as a partner in achieving their goals.

For individuals, this means taking the first step to integrate Generative AI into daily financial routines. Whether it's using an AI-powered app to track expenses or seeking AI-driven investment advice, the possibilities are vast and accessible. For businesses, the journey involves investing in AI infrastructure, training teams to use these tools effectively, and fostering a culture of innovation that encourages experimentation and growth.

Ultimately, the value of Generative AI lies in its ability to empower users. It democratizes access to advanced financial tools, making them available to everyone, regardless of their level of expertise. This inclusivity ensures that the benefits of AI are not confined to a select few but are shared widely, contributing to a more equitable financial landscape.

ENCOURAGING FINANCIAL EMPOWERMENT THROUGH GENERATIVE AI

The journey to financial empowerment is deeply personal and filled with unique challenges. Everyone aspires to achieve financial security, whether it's to live a more fulfilling life, support loved ones, or plan for future endeavors. Yet, the path to financial success can often feel overwhelming, with decisions involving investments, savings, budgeting, and long-term planning requiring precision and clarity. This is where Generative AI steps in as an innovative ally, offering tools and insights that make financial empowerment accessible to everyone.

Embracing Generative AI in your financial strategy doesn't mean replacing your judgment or intuition—it means enhancing your ability to make informed, effective decisions. With its capabilities to analyze patterns, predict trends, and generate tailored solutions, Generative AI can provide the support and resources needed to take control of your financial future.

Building Confidence in Financial Decisions

One of the most intimidating aspects of financial management is the fear of making the wrong decision. Many people hesitate to invest, save, or even create a budget because they feel unsure about the outcomes. Generative AI helps reduce this uncertainty by providing actionable insights that are backed by data. Whether you're deciding where to invest your money, how to allocate your savings, or whether to take on a new financial commitment, AI tools can offer clear guidance based on your unique circumstances.

Imagine having a virtual assistant that can predict market trends, simulate various investment scenarios, or recommend a personalized savings plan tailored to your needs. This kind of support not only builds confidence but also empowers individuals to act decisively. By using AI tools, you are no longer navigating the complexities of finance alone—you have a powerful partner guiding you every step of the way.

Personalizing Financial Goals

Every individual's financial journey is different. Some people aim to retire early, while others prioritize saving for their children's education or building a safety net for unexpected expenses. Generative AI thrives on personalization. It analyzes your financial habits, preferences, and goals to create strategies tailored specifically for you.

For instance, if you're focused on long-term savings, Generative

AI can suggest dynamic plans that adapt as your income or expenses change. If you're interested in ethical investments, it can identify opportunities aligned with your values. This level of customization ensures that your financial plans are not just effective but also deeply meaningful to you.

Simplifying Complex Financial Processes

Managing finances often involves juggling multiple tasks, including monitoring expenses, filing taxes, and planning for future milestones. The complexity of these tasks can deter people from taking proactive steps toward financial empowerment. Generative AI simplifies these processes by automating routine tasks and offering intuitive solutions.

For example, instead of manually tracking expenses and categorizing them, AI tools can do it for you in real time. They can identify spending patterns, highlight areas for improvement, and even suggest ways to optimize your budget. When it comes to taxes, Generative AI can analyze deductions, calculate liabilities, and ensure compliance with the latest regulations—all while saving you hours of effort.

By handling these time-consuming tasks, AI frees up your energy to focus on bigger-picture financial goals. This simplification makes it easier to take consistent, positive steps toward financial success without feeling overwhelmed by the details.

Bridging the Knowledge Gap

Financial literacy is a crucial component of financial empowerment; however, many people struggle to understand complex financial concepts. Generative AI bridges this gap by presenting information in a clear and actionable manner. Instead of relying on generic advice or wading through dense financial jargon, you can access insights that are directly relevant to your needs.

For instance, if you're new to investing, AI tools can explain the basics while also providing specific recommendations tailored to your risk tolerance and goals. If you're exploring retirement planning, they can project your future needs and suggest realistic strategies to achieve them. This combination of education and practical application empowers individuals to make decisions with clarity and confidence.

Creating Opportunities for Everyone

Generative AI democratizes access to financial tools and strategies that were once reserved for those with significant wealth or expertise. In the past, hiring a financial advisor or gaining access to cutting-edge financial insights often required considerable resources. Today, AI-powered platforms make these services accessible to a wider audience.

For individuals with limited financial knowledge or resources, this is a game-changer. Generative AI offers the opportunity to build wealth, manage risks, and achieve financial security, regardless of one's starting point. It levels the playing field, ensuring that everyone has an equal opportunity to succeed.

For instance, small business owners can use AI to streamline their financial operations, identify cost-saving opportunities, and plan for growth. Similarly, individuals from diverse backgrounds can access tools that help them navigate complex financial systems with ease. This inclusivity is a powerful step toward broader financial empowerment.

Encouraging a Growth Mindset

Embracing Generative AI also fosters a growth mindset in financial management. Instead of viewing finances as a fixed, daunting challenge, you can approach them as an evolving journey of learning and improvement. AI tools offer continuous feedback, enabling you to adapt to changes in your circumstances or the broader financial landscape.

For example, if your income increases, Generative AI can suggest ways to allocate the extra funds toward investments, savings, or other goals. If market conditions shift, it can help you adjust your strategies to minimize risks and capitalize on opportunities. This adaptability fosters resilience and confidence, enabling you to navigate uncertainties with ease.

Enhancing Financial Security

Financial security is a cornerstone of empowerment. Generative AI contributes to this by offering robust tools for risk management and fraud prevention. It can monitor your accounts for unusual activity, identify potential vulnerabilities in your financial plans, and recommend proactive measures to protect your assets.

For instance, AI tools can detect subtle patterns that may indicate fraud, alerting you before significant damage occurs. They can also analyze your financial habits to identify areas of risk, such as over-reliance on a single income source or insufficient emergency savings. By addressing these vulnerabilities, Generative AI enables you to build a stronger and more secure financial foundation.

Inspiring Proactive Engagement

One of the most empowering aspects of Generative AI is its ability to inspire proactive engagement with your finances. Instead of reacting to financial challenges as they arise, you can take a forward-thinking approach to planning and decision-making. AI tools encourage this mindset by providing real-time insights and actionable recommendations.

For example, rather than waiting until the end of the year to review your budget, you can use AI to monitor and adjust it on an ongoing basis. Instead of making last-minute investment decisions based on market trends, you can rely on AI-driven forecasts to plan. This proactive engagement not only enhances financial outcomes but also instills a sense of control and empowerment.

Building a Legacy

Financial empowerment is not just about achieving your own goals—it's also about creating a lasting impact for future generations. Generative AI can support this by helping you plan for long-term objectives, such as retirement, education funds, or estate planning. By providing clear, actionable strategies, AI ensures that your financial legacy is secure and meaningful.

For instance, if you want to leave an inheritance for your children, AI tools can help you calculate the necessary savings, investments, and insurance coverage. If you're passionate about philanthropy, they can recommend ways to maximize your charitable contributions while preserving your financial stability. This level of planning empowers you to make decisions that align with your values and aspirations.

Empowerment Through Action

Ultimately, the true power of Generative AI lies in its ability to inspire action. Understanding its capabilities is only the first step—embracing and applying them is what leads to real transformation. By integrating AI into your financial journey, you can take meaningful steps toward achieving your goals, whether they involve building wealth, reducing debt, or simply gaining peace of mind.

Generative AI is not just a tool—it's a partner in your pursuit of financial empowerment. It offers the knowledge, support, and resources needed to turn aspirations into reality. By leveraging its potential, you can navigate the complexities of finance with confidence, clarity, and purpose.

As you move forward, remember that financial empowerment is an ongoing process. It requires curiosity, adaptability, and a willingness to embrace new tools and strategies. Generative AI provides the foundation for this journey, offering insights and solutions that make every step more manageable and rewarding.

By choosing to leverage Generative AI, you are taking a bold step toward a brighter financial future. The possibilities are endless, and the growth potential is limitless. All it takes is the decision to begin—and the confidence to continue.

REFERENCES

1. Choudhury, S., & Patel, R. 2021. AI and Wealth Management: A New Era of Personalized Finance. Springer.
2. Davenport, T. H., & Ronanki, R. 2018. "Artificial Intelligence for the Real World." Harvard Business Review.
3. Goldberg, Alec. 2024. "AI in Finance: Leveraging Large Language Models for Enhanced Decision-Making and Risk Management." Social Science Journal For Advanced Research, July Issue.
4. Gonzalo Martínez, Lauren Watson, Pedro Reviriego, José Alberto Hernández, Marc Juarez, Rik Sarkar. 2024. Epistemic Uncertainty in Artificial Intelligence.
5. Heeks, R. 2001. Understanding E-Governance For Development.
6. Huang, K. 2023. "Generative AI in Finance: The New Frontier for Wealth Management." Journal of Financial Technology, 19(4) 123-135.
7. Huang, K., Wang, Y., Zhang, X. 2024. Generative AI Security, Future of Business and Finance. Springer, Cham.
8. Joel Jebadurai Devapitchai, Krishnapriya S. V., Karuppiah S. P., William Robert P., S. Saranya. 2024. Generative AI for Transformational Management.
9. Kapoor, A., & Chaudhury, P. 2022. Wealth Management in the Digital Age: Strategies for Financial Success. Wiley.

10. Kholoud Aldous, Joni Salminen, Ali Farooq, Soon-Gyo Jung, Bernard Jansen. 2024. Using ChatGPT in Content Marketing: Enhancing Users' Social Media Engagement in Cross-Platform Content Creation through Generative AI.
11. Kun-Hsien Lin, Cheng-An Shen, Su-Chuan Cheng. 2024. "Applications of AI in Digital Governance Services for Local Taxes- a case of the Local Tax Bureau of Taichung City Government." Proceedings of the 25th Annual International Conference on Digital Government Research 6 - 18.
12. Lopez-Lira, Alejandro. 2024. The Predictive Edge: Outsmart the Market using Generative AI and ChatGPT in Financial Forecasting. John Wiley & Sons.
13. Manu, Alexander. 2024. Generative AI as a Disruptor. Chapman and Hall/CRC.
14. Mousa Al-Kfairy, Dheya Mustafa, Nir Kshetri, Mazen Insiew, Omar Alfandi. 2024. "Ethical Challenges and Solutions of Generative AI: An Interdisciplinary Perspective." Social Informatics and Digital Humanities.
15. Pattyam, Sandeep Pushyamitra. 2024. "AI-Driven Financial Market Analysis: Advanced Techniques for Stock Price Prediction, Risk Management, and Automated Trading." African J. of Artificial Int. and Sust. Dev., vol. 1 100–135.
16. Pooya Azadi, Sudhir Krishnamurthi. 2024. Integrating Generative AI Into Investment Processes. Washington, D.C..
17. Pouyan Parsafard, Ogerta Elezaj, Damilola Ekundayo and

Edlira Vakaj . 2024. Automation in Construction Cost Budgeting using Generative Artificial Intelligence. IEOM Society International, USA.

18. Rane, Nitin. 2023. Role and Challenges of ChatGPT and Similar Generative Artificial Intelligence in Finance and Accounting.

19. 2024. "Retirement Financial Planning: Strategies and Challenges in Avoiding the Incidence of Poverty." Artificial Intelligence (AI) and Customer Social Responsibility (CSR) 101–109.

20. Roger, Jianglin Dennis Ding. 2024. "AI-Driven Financial Modeling Techniques: Transforming Investment Strategies." The Journal of Applied Business and Economics, Vol. 26, 63-74.

21. Shrestha, Rasu. 2024. "Embracing Generative AI: Transforming Health Care Through Innovation and Human Connection." NEJM Catalyst.

22. Smith, T. R. 2023. Artificial Intelligence for Investment Professionals. CFA Institute.

23. Soraya Sedkaoui, Rafika Benaichouba. 2024. "Generative AI as a transformative force for innovation: a review of opportunities, applications and challenges." European Journal of Innovation Management.

24. Subramanyam Sahoo, Kamlesh Dutta. 2024. "Boardwalk Empire: How Generative AI is Revolutionizing Economic Paradigms."

25. Vasquez, R. & Chen, W. 2022. "Generative Models for Financial Forecasting: Applications and Implications." Journal of Financial Engineering 76-89.
26. Westerman, G., & Bonnet, D. 2019. "Predicting the Organizational Impact of Artificial Intelligence." MIT Sloan Management Review.
27. Xukang Wang; Ying Cheng Wu. 2024. "Balancing Innovation and Regulation in the Age of Generative Artificial Intelligence." Journal of Information Policy.

AUTHOR **PROFILE**

Oladipupo Jude Mesole is very passionate about using *Artificial Intelligence* to improve human life, which inspired the writing of this book to help readers improve their finances. Prior to writing this book, the Author successfully designed an AI system to evaluate risk of cardiovascular disease in the United Kingdom in 2013, He previously worked as an **Information Technology** specialist in the **Banking sector** and **Real estate**, He worked with Multinational corporations as a consultant such as **KPMG, SAP, Hunters Group, Prologis UK**,

He graduated from the Federal University of Technology Minna, with a **Bachelor of Technology degree in Physics/ Telecommunications in 2006**, an **MSc in Computer Engineering (Software Systems)** from the University of East London in 2013, **A Doctor of Theology Degree** from Christ Life Bible institute and seminary New York, in year 2020, a **PGP in Data Analytics** from Purdue University, 2021, and a **PGP in Applied Generative AI** from Purdue University 2024.

He is a **Certified SAP Business Process Consultant in SAP SD** from Waldorf Germany in 2013, Certified Data Analyst, USA 2021, and **Certified Applied Generative AI** (USA) 2024.

Oladipupo Jude Mesole is currently undertaking his PhD in Organizational Leadership with research on Physicians' Perception of Ethical Leadership in the Deployment of Generative AI in healthcare at Columbia International University.

www.ingramcontent.com/pod-product-compliance
Lightning Source LLC
LaVergne TN
LVHW050908210926
848482LV00012B/376
* 9 7 9 8 2 9 5 5 2 9 9 4 8 *